Harnessing the Nine Hallmarks of Aging

Harnessing the Nine Hallmarks of Aging

By Greg Macpherson

With Adrienne Kohler

ISBN: 978-0-473-56892-4

Dedication

To Casey, Connor, Sophie and Jack—Thank you for all your patience and support whilst I completed this project. Even one extra day on this planet with you will be a bonus—but let's aim for decades.

"Greg Macpherson has written the best book on anti-aging I have ever seen! It is easy to read, extremely detailed and offers so many important and well researched data that we can apply to our daily lives. Each chapter is ripe with new insights on ways in which we can begin now to turn back the clock. This book is a must read and will be the best investment you will ever make!"

Dr. John P. Salerno

Medical Director, Salerno Center New York City

I've been waiting a long time for a comprehensive yet user-friendly book on slowing the aging process and science-based ideas to living longer with optimal functionality. Greg's book is now the ultimate resource on the topic. Get a copy for yourself and bring one to your doctor.

Dr. Geo Espinosa

Naturopathic Functional Medicine doctor, Faculty at New York University Langone Health, Creator of DrGeo.com

"Graceful aging with both quality and quantity are mankind's highest goal. Greg has created a simplified yet scientific masterpiece that provides a path to this mystical yet achievable goal. My the wisdom in this book give you the life that you want and deserve."

Mark C. Houston MD MS MSC

Director of Hypertension Institute, Nashville, Tennessee

"Great strides have been made by attacking heart disease, cancer and other potentially lethal conditions. Much needs to be done to conquer the fundamental biology of aging which is the soil these chronic disease grow in. Mr. Macpherson presents in a masterful yet approachable manner an important work that aging can be understood and approach at its origins to improve our lives and those of our loved ones. I recommend this book with the highest accolades"

Joel Kahn, MD, FACC

Clinical Professor of Medicine Author, "The Plant Based Solution"

"It was indeed a pleasure reading Greg Macpherson's book on anti-aging medicine. This is a definite eye opener packed with the most leading and cutting edge information. Everyone needs to assimilate the author's solutions and insights regarding the dreaded consequences of accelerated aging and premature illness that weakens modern man. Although some complex genetic information regarding inflammation and toxicity is presented, the author does this in a unique, easy to read fashion. Yes, this book is as contemporary as it gets! And the information will add years to your life. A great read!"

Stephen T. Sinatra, MD, FACC, FACN
ASSISTANT CLINICAL PROFESSOR OF MEDICINE UNIVERSITY OF CONNECTICUT, SCHOOL OF MEDICINE FARMINGTON, CT

Greg Macpherson has brought to bear his expertise in the pharmaceutical and nutritional sciences to lay out a comprehensive state of the science in the emerging field of healthy aging. His description of the hallmarks of aging is clear, complete, and fascinating while his advice on applying the best knowledge we have to your own life is practical and actionable. A must read for people interested in the new science of aging

Greg Horn
NUTRITION INNOVATOR AND BEST-SELLING AUTHOR OF LIVING GREEN AND LIVING WELL.

FOREWORD

When passion, clinical experience, and science meet, you realize something special has been created. It is an honor to write this foreword for my esteemed colleague that has captured the pearls that every human being is walking this planet needs to understand and infuse into their life's journey and those they love.

As you read Greg's book, the reader quickly realizes the depth of research, insight, and power contained within these pages. No longer do you have to accept the aging process of your parents and grandparents. Life is meant to be lived proactively and should be full of vim and vigor throughout the entirety of one's years.

Imagine for a moment transforming your mindset from what has been accepted as a "normal" decline of mind and body as the decades pass to a firm proclamation; I will not embrace getting old and passively accepting maladies of aging!

Greg masterfully imparts years of research and clinical experience into well-organized chapters that describe how you can take charge of the over controllable factors that, if left unchecked, can accelerate biological aging. You no longer need to be in the dark on how to actively manage DNA methylation, autophagy, glycation, mitochondrial dysfunction, mTOR, and countless other biochemical processes to add health to trillions of cells that comprise your very essence.

I can honestly say, as an author of 18 health and wellness books and 200 published clinical articles, I was excited to learn and appreciate the nuances of how to integrate the proactive steps that Greg lays out for my pursuit of living a young and vital life for the decades to come. This masterpiece puts you in charge of not having to accept your chronological age on your birth certificate.

I applaud Greg for his ability to reduce complex concepts into very understandable actionable steps that can be pursued and employed to take charge of your wellness trajectory. Today is the beginning of the metamorphosis that your body has been waiting for; regardless of your initial knowledge of longevity medicine, you will be left in awe and inspired.

May you be blessed abundantly,

Dr. Chris D. Meletis

International Author, Lecturer,
and Educator of Physicians

Contents

INTRODUCTION

A NEW PARADIGM OF AGING

The idea is to die young as late as possible.

–ASHLEY MONTAGU

A Life Well Lived

In June 2020, American actor, director, and comedian Carl Reiner died at age 98. Born in 1922, he began working at 16, started his career in entertainment during World War II, and for the next seven decades worked across all aspects of show business. He wrote the last edition of his memoirs in 2015, and up to his death he was sharing political commentary and entertainment insights with his 385,000 followers on Twitter. In the days before he died, he took part in a virtual recreation of the movie, *The Princess Bride.* It was not quite a century, but by any reckoning, it was a life well-lived.

It is also a life worth emulating. Regrettably, for many people, growing old is a frightening prospect, so what I want to do with this book is to help you make a fundamental change in how you think about aging so you too can have a life well-lived.

I want to help redefine what it means to age in an approaching era when many people can expect to live to a very old age and give you the advice and tools to help reduce the risk of chronic disease so you can live your best life possible for as long as possible.

However, before we begin, I want you to consider your attitude about aging.

- How does the prospect of living an extended life to 100 and maybe beyond make you feel? Happy and excited, or anxious and fearful?
- If it makes you fearful, at what age did you worrying about getting old?
- Do you see yourself healthy or unhealthy in your old age?
- What do you do in your daily routine to prepare yourself mentally, physically, and financially for living a long life?

If you view aging positively, that's wonderful, but if you are like most people, the thought of aging probably makes you anxious or even fearful. Do you see yourself in old age as being frail and sickly, waiting for death? You may have plans for your financial retirement, but how much thought have you given to your health and physical well-being?

My challenge to you is to become excited about the prospect of living in good health for eighty, ninety, even a hundred years and beyond. Imagine what you could do with that time? Envision having not just one but several further careers, pursuing a myriad of interests, and watching your grandchildren and even your great-grandchildren grow up.

I want you to imagine a scenario where you enjoy accumulating wisdom over the years rather than maladies.

In the chapters ahead, I will discuss how and why we age so you understand the biological and social factors you will need to consider throughout your life. Then, I will offer strategies you can use to build an individualized life plan that will act as a guide to help you live and age in the best health possible.

As you will discover, our bodies are incredible and dynamic molecular machines, and nothing is set in stone. We can influence the aging process more than we think with a few simple choices and lifestyle changes that can make a dramatic difference to your health and how well you age.

CHAPTER 1
HOW LONG CAN WE LIVE?

THE HUMAN LIFE SPAN

Carl Reiner's life was worth emulating in another way. At 98, he lived 20 years longer than the average life expectancy for a male in the United States, which currently is 78.6 years[1], but he was about two decades shy of the possible human life span.

The Limits of The Human Life Span

Life span and life expectancy are not the same and often confused. The life span of an organism is the *longest possible time* they can live, while life expectancy is the time an organism is *expected to live* based on their environment and lifestyle factors.

Think of life span as how high it is possible a human to jump as opposed to how high a person can *actually* jump. Currently, the highest recorded standing jump is 1.53 meters (5ft 5 in) on average, most people can only jump about one meter (3 ft) high.

The human life span today is about 120 years, but there are two schools of thought (and fierce argument) among longevity researchers whether humans have yet to hit their maximum life span. Some say we have, while others insist it is still an open question.[21]

To date, the longest-lived human being was Frenchwoman Jeanne Calment, who was born in 1875 and lived to be 122 years old. The next oldest was American Sarah Knauss, who lived to 119 and died in December 1999. However, these two are outliers as the bulk of super-centenarians (people who live past 110) usually only live to about 117. To reach this advanced old age is still extremely rare with fewer than 1700 super-centenarians verified through history.[3]

This has led some researchers to assert that the natural human lifespan is limited, placing it at about 115 years old. The evidence for this, they say, is that although human life expectancy has risen sharply since the late 18th century, there has been no significant increase in the maximum recorded age of death since the 1990s.[4]

Other researchers, such as biologist and professor of genetics David Sinclair, believe that an upper limit to the human lifespan has yet to be reached.[5] [2]

Life Expectancy Over Human History

While the potential human life span is still and open and a fascinating question, our interest lies in **life expectancy**. This is based on the age a particular population group will be on average when they die. This means it varies greatly, dependent on factors as location, health systems, gender and occupation.

For most of human history, the average life expectancy at was rarely above 40, and in 1800, the global life expectancy at birth was around 28 years.[6]

---

2 The debate over the maximum human life span is a fascinating one and worthy of its own book. Scientists such as biologist and professor of genetics David Sinclair believe we have yet to reach our limits, but it does raise many ethical questions.

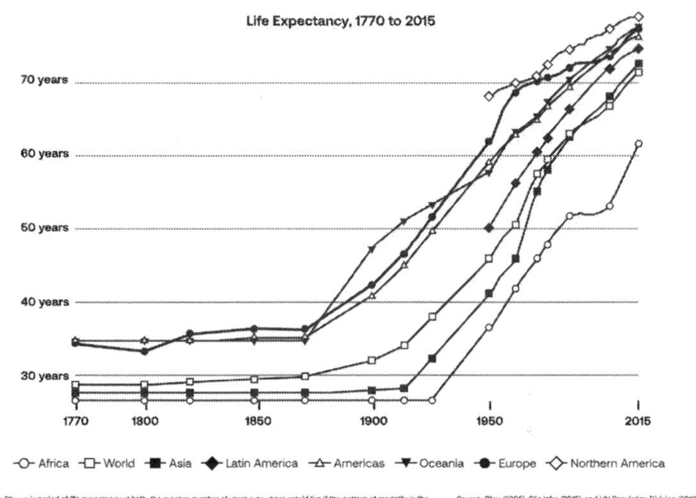

However, this doesn't mean that the most people died at 28 as the average is driven down by high levels of infant and child deaths. Up to the 1900s, more than a third of all children died before the age of five, and most parents could expect to lose two to three of their children.[7 8]

Nonetheless, if they survived the perils of childhood, infectious diseases, and trauma then many people lived well into their 60s and 70s. For example, Greek philosopher Plato was well into his 80s when he died in AD 347, and royalty throughout history lived similar lifespans.[3]

Yet, being rich and noble was no guarantee of a long life, and the aristocracy succumbed to disease and high rates of child mortality as much as the poorer folk.

Life expectancy is also heavily influenced by other factors. For example, it plunged during the 14th century

---

3 Getting accurate records is a major hurdle for information on life expectancy, but because the birth and death of a royalty was of paramount importance, they were usually well documented.

when the Black Death killed a third of Europe's population, and at time of writing, the COVID-19 pandemic has already caused the average US life expectancy to drop.[9]

The Rapid Rise of Human Life Expectancy

The start of the 20th century saw a dramatic change in human life expectancy, and it rose at an accelerated pace, driven by cleaner water supplies, better sanitation, socioeconomic improvements, and vaccination.[10] The surge was checked by the huge death tolls caused by World War I and the Spanish Flu pandemic, but powered ahead again in the 1930s and 40s, driven by the introduction of antibiotics, more vaccines, safer blood transfusions, and many other advances, medical and non-medical.[11]

Not only were fewer people dying young, but more were living to very old age (80 and older). Prior to 1900, living to be 100 was thought to be exceedingly rare. A Danish study found that only three people could reasonably be verified as having lived to 100 in Denmark in each year of the 1870s.[12]

Since 1950, however, the number of people hitting a century has doubled every decade. According to the New England Centenarian Study, (the largest comprehensive study of centenarians in the world) the prevalence rate of centenarians today is about one per 6,000, compared to one per 10,000 when the study began in 1994, making centenarians one of the fastest growing demographics in the global population.[13]

> *Centenarians are one of the fastest growing demographics in the global population*

If this trend continues at the same pace, anyone born since 2000 in countries that have long life expectancy has a very high chance of celebrating their 100th birthday. Moreover, it's feasible with continuing medical advancements and improved awareness of anti-aging strategies, people born over the next few decades may live considerably beyond this.

Our Aging Population

This rapid acceleration in life expectancy has caused one of the most dramatic changes in human civilization. For eons, humans lived in societies of the young, but that is rapidly changing. By 2050 it is expected that Earth will be home to 9.7 billion people. The number of people aged 60 and is expected to double by 2050 and then more than triple by 2100, rising from 962 million globally in 2017 to 2.1 billion in 2050 and 3.1 billion by 2100.[14]

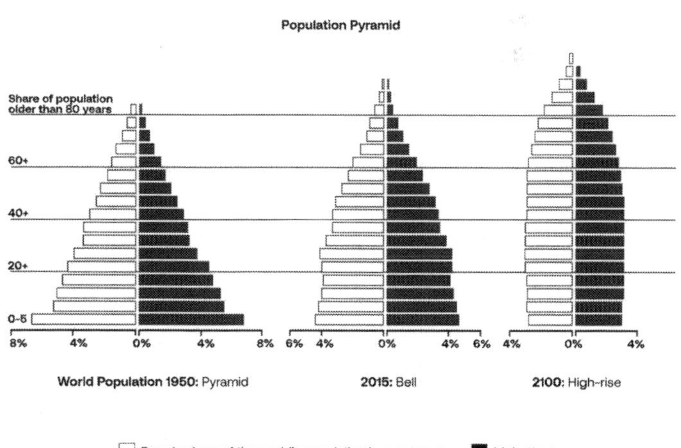

In Europe, 25 percent of the population is already over 60 and projected to reach 35 percent in 2050, before leveling out in the second half of the century.

Other regions are also expected to age significantly over the next century to 2100. Africa has the youngest age distribution of any region, and will remain relatively young for several more decades, but by 2100 people aged 60 and over will reach nearly 20 percent.

From a Pyramid to a Rectangle

This impact of this aging population is already being felt in many countries. One measure that reveals the effect of this is the **potential support ratio (PSR)**, which compares the numbers of people of working age (15- 64) to those over 65.

This ratio is already falling around the world. For the US, the ratio in 1950 was 7:9, that is 7 people of working age for 9 people aged over 65.

In 2020 the ratio has fallen to 3.9, meaning there are now just under 4 people of working age for every 1 person over the age of 65.

Despite living longer, we are not yet living healthier for longer

In Japan, which has one of the longest life expectancies in the world, this ratio is now 1.8, meaning there are just under 2 people of working age for every one over 65.

In countries with large younger populations, such as Kenya, the ratio is completely reversed, at about 5:1.

By 2050, many countries, mostly in Europe, Northern America, and Eastern and South-Eastern Asia, expect to have such low PSRs that labor markets and the economy will suffer from not enough people to fill jobs or support the elderly.[15]

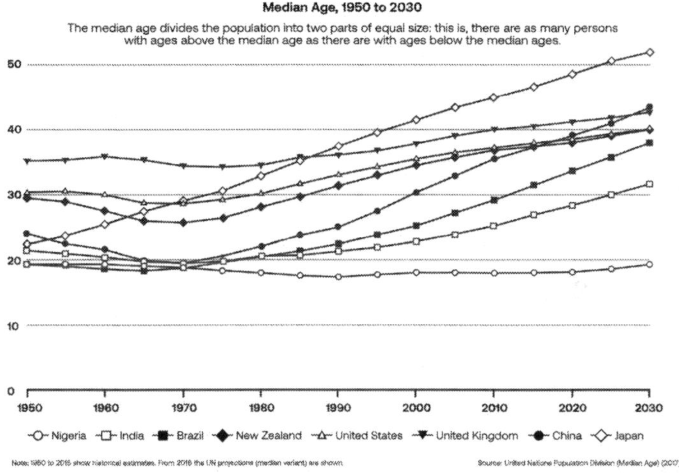

This changing population structure will also stress the health systems needed to care for such a large population of older people because, despite living longer, we are not yet living healthier for longer. Unless we change this, we face a future where many people will spend the last few decades of their life in ill-health, struggling to afford care or have someone to help them.

Summary

There is a sizeable gap between the potential human life span, which is about 117 years, and life expectancy at about 79 years. However, our life expectancy has rapidly climbed since 1900, when it was only about 40 years, driven by medical and non-medical advancements.

As many people can expect to reach advanced old age, this rapid growth is changing the structure of human populations, with a higher proportion of older people and fewer people of working age to support them. In coming years, this will negatively affect economies and health care systems globally if we don't prepare for this change.

Chapter 2
Closing the Disease Gap

Changing Our Future

The key to changing our future is improving our **health span**–the period of our life we spend in good health, free from the chronic or serious diseases and disabilities of aging.[1]

***Health span**–the period of our life we spend in good health, free from the chronic or serious diseases and disabilities of aging*

Conversely, our **disease span** is the number of years we live with illnesses that interfere with our quality of living. These are usually diseases of aging and they tend to develop in clusters, meaning as we age, we can get more than one, including cardiovascular disease, arthritis, diabetes, cancer, and dementia.[1]

Unlike the average life expectancy, for many years there was no way to measure the length of the average health span. To address this, the World Health Organization (WHO) developed an indicator, called the **HALE–Healthy Life Expectancy.**[2] This calculates how long we can expect

[1] This concept known as multi-morbidity

to live in good health. Currently, the global HALE at birth for males and females combined is **63.1 years**, while the HALE at birth ranges from a low of **51.1 years** for African males to **70.5 years** for females in Europe.[3]

This means there is, on average, a ten-year gap for most people between time they can expect to live in good health and when they die.

This is the key challenge I want to address–how can we close this gap, so we live as long as possible in the best health possible? To paraphrase the opening quote, so we die old as young as possible.

The inherent problem with merely increasing life expectancy is that it also increases our chances of getting ill simply because we live long enough to succumb to age-related diseases.[4]

Reducing the Health Span Gap

Closing this gap is a major challenge for health agencies worldwide. To address it, the **Global Burden of Disease Study** is a comprehensive regional and global research program that looks at the disease burden from major diseases, injuries, and risk factors.[5]

The latest study details the incidence, prevalence, and years lived with disability (YLDs) for 354 causes in 195 countries and territories from 1990 to 2017.

Unfortunately, what the data from this study shows is that the length of the human health span has barely improved. Although our life expectancy has increased, the relative length of time we spend in ill-health at the end of our lives has barely improved.

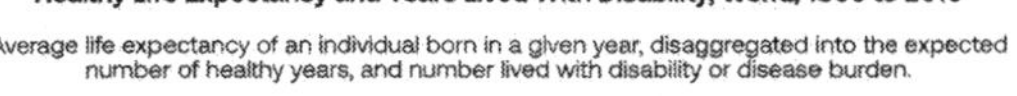

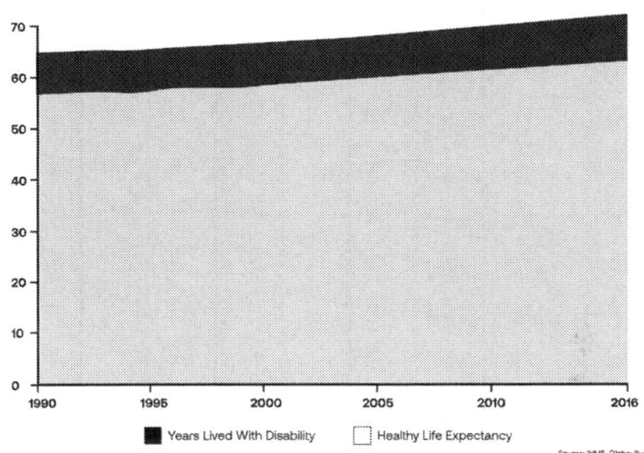

This health gap has huge financial implications for everyone as health costs generally rise as we grow older. In the US, for example, although people over 55 make up less than one third of the population, they account for more than half (56%) of health spending. Meanwhile, people under 35, who make up 46 percent of the population account for less than a quarter of health spending.[6]

If we can reduce or even eliminate the gap between when we become ill and when we die, it gives everyone five or ten extra healthy years

If we can reduce or even eliminate the gap between when we become ill and when we die, it gives everyone five or ten extra healthy years. That time spent in good health reduces health spending and avoids people having to drain their savings or pension funds to pay for healthcare and support.

More importantly, it is pointless to live longer if we just spend the last portion of our lives miserable and sick. By aging well, we get to lead a longer, healthier, and far happier life, which is something we all wish for.

SUMMARY

Our health span is the length of time we can expect to live in good health.

Our disease span is the number of years we can expect to live with illnesses that interfere with our quality of living.

We need to reduce this gap as most health costs come at the end of our lives. However, currently this is at least ten years shorter than the average health span.

The Global Burden of Disease Study is a global initiative by health agencies to reduce this gap and lower the burden on health care resources.

Chapter 3
The Rise of Preventable Disease

How We Die Now

One of the primary reasons we are living longer is because of a major transformation over time of what we die from. Where once infectious, or communicable diseases (CD), were the main cause of death, now non-communicable diseases (NCDs) such as heart disease, stroke and dementia lead the way.

This is good news in one way, as it means we no longer die from a toothache, but the bad news is that NCDs are often chronic, of long duration and, as mentioned before, we can have more than one at a time.

More than **60 percent** of the global burden of disease is now caused by NCDs, 28 percent from communicable, maternal, neonatal and nutritional diseases, and about 10 percent from injuries.[1]

This is a dramatic change from the turn of the 20th century. In the year 1900, infectious diseases such as pneumonia, tuberculosis (TB), diarrhea and enteritis caused a third of all deaths in adults and almost a third of deaths in children under five years old in the USA.[2]

This had changed markedly by 1950 when NCDs such as heart disease and stroke had become the leading causes of death. Today in high-income countries, they account for more than 80 percent of the disease burden. However, this isn't the case in low-income nations, where communicable diseases such as respiratory infections, HIV/AIDS and malaria still cause more than 60 percent of illnesses.

Death by Lifestyle

The tragedy is that non-communicable diseases are usually driven by external forces and mostly preventable. These factors include rapid unplanned urbanization, the globalization of unhealthy lifestyles and diets, and economic disparity.

This interaction of environment and lifestyle affecting our health is evident when we compare how people got sick and died in previous centuries. In 1812, cannonball injuries were a major cause of concern for doctors, while neurasthenia[3], a disorder of "depleted nervous energy" was widely reported in the late 19th century, but has since disappeared.[4 1]

In some cases, a disease's decline clearly-resulted from medical action. Smallpox was feared for centuries and devastated human populations. The first vaccine was discovered by chance in 1776, when an English doctor, Edward Jenner, realized that milkmaids who had contracted cowpox were immune to smallpox.[5] However, it was only in the mid to late twentieth century that a global vaccination campaign run by the WHO successfully eradicated the disease.

Thankfully, another major killer, death in childbirth caused by postpartum infections is rarely seen these days, but it only declined once the medical profession accepted

---

1 According to doctors of the time, "two sorts of persons were particularly at risk of overtaxing their supply of nervous energy: ultracompetitive businessmen and socially active women."

infections were transmitted by birth attendants and started making them wash their hands.[6] [2]

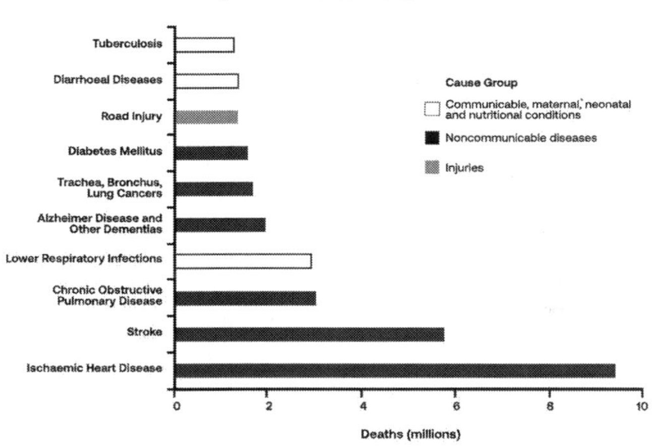

The development of vaccines and antibiotics, and improved sanitation from the 1930s onward greatly reduced our risk of dying from infections. This was followed by effective treatments and cures for diseases such as pneumonia, tuberculosis, and gastrointestinal infections. But this means that although people live longer, we now live long enough to fall victim to diseases of aging such as heart attacks, stroke, and dementia.

> *Although people live longer, we now live long enough to fall victim to diseases of aging such as heart attacks, stroke, and dementia.*

---

2 From the 1600s through the mid-to-late 1800s, most childbed post-partum infections were caused by the doctors carrying germs from one patient to the next.

Incidence vs Prevalence

Before we go further, I want to define the difference **incidence** and **prevalence** as this is important to grasp.

Incidence conveys information about *the risk of getting a disease*, whereas **prevalence** is a measure of *how many people have the disease.*

So, to understand why more people seem to be suffering from a disease, it is important to find out whether the incidence rate is rising or if it is more prevalent.

As people no longer die young from infections, they now live long enough to have a heart attack, so the **prevalence** rate of heart disease has risen as life expectancy has increased.

This means older people are suffering more heart attacks or stroke simply because there are more of them. Meanwhile, **incidence rates** have stayed stable for some diseases, with the rate for attacks and strokes declining even though they are now a leading cause of death.

In other words, if the incidence rate is one per 1000 and there are only 1000 old people, then 1 person would die. However, if there is 10,000 old people, then 10 people would die.

The Good News

This is actually good news, as our success at overcoming infectious diseases means we have the power to reduce the impact of non-communicable diseases.

The main barrier we face to living a long healthy life is addressing the lifestyle and environmental factors that cause them and reduce our health span. In the next chapter I am going to examine the most fundamental–our fear of aging and why it is a myth.

SUMMARY

As medical advances improved treatment of infectious disease (communicable disease) and increased life expectancy, more of us now live long enough to develop non communicable diseases (NCDs) including chronic diseases of aging.

Diseases of aging often come in clusters, a concept called multi-morbidity.

60 percent of the global burden of disease is caused by NCDs, 28 percent from communicable, maternal, neonatal and nutritional diseases, and about 10 percent from injuries.

Factors driving NCDs include rapid unplanned urbanization, the globalization of unhealthy lifestyles and diets, and economic disparity.

Incidence rates of some diseases like stroke and heart attack are falling, but prevalence rates are rising because of more older people.

Chapter 4

Agism And the Cult of Youth

For centuries, humans have pursued ways to stay young and prolong their life, from Chinese emperors drinking elixirs of immortality containing toxic chemicals, to Romans and nobles throughout time plastering their faces with lead makeup to maintain an illusion of youth (and poisoning themselves in the process).[1]

So where does this fear of aging come from? Our concept of aging is largely a social construct. Although advertisers, marketers, and sociologists like to slice and dice the human life span into rigid demographics, our life span is a continuum with huge variances in how we develop and grow. Chronological and biological age varies widely among individuals, influenced by a complex interaction of genes, environment, and behavior.

Actors and musicians are a useful way to see this variance at work because their lives are spent in the public eye and often documented from an early age.

The popular image of a-74-year-old women is old and bent, frail, maybe working in her garden or sitting in her chair watching TV at a retirement village. Compare that image to actress and singer Cher, who in 2020 at 74, continues to act, sing, and tour her Las Vegas show.

---

1 The use of lead makeup was prized in ancient times and continued to be used in cosmetics up to modern times, even though its ill-effects were well-known.

Granted, even today few 74-year-olds look like Cher, but it shows what is possible. Growing old is not what it used to be.

What Is Old?

Life stages are fluid, yet humanity seems determined to focus on a few short years at our prime—roughly 18 to 25—and spend the rest of our considerable lives trying to create a facsimile of youth instead of enjoying each year and stage of life as it arises.

If we break down our lives, using 50 as the midpoint, then we will spend the same amount of time (and more of our adult lives) living after 50 than the years before. Surely it makes sense to spend this time as constructively and in the best health that we can.

0 to 13 Childhood | 13 to 40 Early adulthood | 40 to 100 Adulthood

The Invention of Life Stages

Even the concepts of life stages are relatively modern, particularly that of middle-age, which only emerged in the early 1900s and gained traction after World War I. According to author Patricia Cohen in her book *In Our Prime*,[1] a combination of the disillusionment that followed WWI, the growth of the Hollywood film industry, and mass consumerism "conspired to create a cult of youth" which led to life-stages being rigidly defined by marketers and government agencies.

Anyone who turns 55 these days will be all too familiar with the tsunami of retirement village and funeral insurance advertisements that descend upon them, driven by social media algorithms that define anyone over 55 as 'old'.

Moreover, our individual perceptions of aging change with each generation. Think of your parents when they were the same age as you are now and how you view yourself. How did they seem to you at the time? Most likely you consider yourself to be much younger (at least in spirit) than you thought them at the time.

Unfortunately, humans have trapped themselves in a conundrum. Everyone ages, yet so many of us fear old age. We are bombarded with negative stereotypes of aging, depicting it as a time of loneliness and constant illness, and these views are often held by both younger and older people. The consequences of this on our health can be dire as numerous studies have shown that one of the best ways to age well is to have a positive view of aging, and that a negative view can influence our physical and mental health well-being for the worse.[2]

The High Cost of Agism

Researchers at the Yale School of Public Health undertook a global analysis of the health consequences of age-based discrimination as part of a wider WHO campaign to combat agism. They examined 422 studies covering seven million people from 45 countries spanning the globe. All these studies found evidence of systemic agism.

This systemic negative bias against aging operates at a structural level (for example, employment opportunities) and at an individual level, it acts in three main and interrelated ways:

- Age discrimination (detrimental treatment of older people)
- Negative age stereotypes (beliefs about older people in general)

- Negative self-perceptions of aging (beliefs held by older people about their own aging)

Four of these effects were at the structural level:

- Denial of access to health care
- Exclusion from clinical trials
- Having resources, including medical services, rationed because of age
- Limited work opportunities

Seven at the individual level:

- Decreased longevity
- Poorer quality of life
- Compromised social relationships
- Risky health behaviors
- Mental illness
- Cognitive impairment
- Physical illnesses

This global negative reinforcement of agism was found to have serious physical and mental consequences for many people:

- Older people were excluded from medical trials of diseases that affected them, including half of the clinical trials for Parkinson's disease (PD) even though this is more prevalent in later life.
- Workplace agism worsened health and increased symptoms of depression and long-term illness.
- Employers were far less likely to hire older job applicants or offer access to training.
- Those who faced agism in the workplace were more likely to retire early, while employers (especially British and US) were more likely to

place older employees in positions with lower pay and responsibility than younger employees with similar qualifications.

- Older people with more negative self-perceptions of aging had a significantly reduced life span.
- More than 6 million older people experience depression globally due to agism.
- When older persons resisted negative age stereotypes, they were less likely to experience suicidal thoughts, anxiety, and PTSD.
- Older people who experienced high levels of agism were less likely to undertake health-promoting behaviors, worsening their physical wellbeing.
- Older persons with negative self-perceptions of aging or assimilated negative age stereotypes from society were more likely to have functional decline or dementia compared to those who assimilated positive age stereotypes.

Our Fear of Getting Old

It was Pulitzer Prize-winning activist and aging pioneer Dr. Robert Butler, who first coined the terms agism and longevity revolution. He recognized discrimination against the elderly as early as 1968, and in 1975 he became the founding director of the US National Institute on Aging of the National Institutes of Health.

"Overall, in 95.5% of the 422 studies reviewed, agism predicted significantly worse health outcomes and impacted the health of people in all of the countries studied."

In his 2009 book, *The Longevity Revolution*[3] he attributes our underlying universal fear of aging to a dread and fear of growing older, becoming ill and dependent as we age, and an inability to accept our mortality

"*One of the striking facts of human life is the intensity with which people avoid aging.* Narcissistic *preoccupation with our own aging and demise and perhaps, according to Freud, the inability of the unconscious to accept death make it difficult for society as a whole to deal with the challenges of aging.*"

Butler said systemic agism leads the health-care system, and even individuals, to disregard or neglect illnesses such as joint pain or high blood pressure because doctors see them as part of the natural process of aging instead of as treatable conditions.

This can cause needless suffering. For example, more than 50 conditions can cause or mimic the symptoms of dementia. Two common ones are caused by a vitamin B12 deficiency or an underactive thyroid (hypothyroidism), and memory impairment caused by depression and infections.

In a follow-up study by the Yale team, they found that agism in the US instigated 17 million cases a year of the eight most expensive health conditions for people aged over 60, leading to excess costs of $63 billion per year in that country alone.[4]

According to Butler, tackling agism and increasing our health span will take more than good genes, money and access to health care. It will also require us taking individual responsibility and a lifetime perspective of our health and well-being.

Staying in good health for as long as possible reduces the cost of longevity to ourselves and society, increases the contributions we can make to society and the satisfaction we experience in life and, as we discuss later in the chapter on epigenetics, can even flow to our descendants through our genes and help them lead healthier lives.

The good news is that cultural beliefs about aging are just that—beliefs—and beliefs can change.

What if we can live longer and healthier by pushing back the diseases of aging or never experiencing them at all? The goal is not to live forever; the goal is to stay healthier for longer and replace the fear of aging with enthusiasm for living life to its full potential.

The paradox is that agism is prejudice against our future selves. We all age, it is inescapable, and by ignoring it we make our own lives harder.

Summary

How we perceive aging is largely a social construct, as chronological and biological age varies among individuals, influenced by a complex interaction of genes, environment, and behavior.

Life stages are fluid and as we spend most of our adult life after 50, we should try to live in the best health possible.

Agism exists in almost all societies and leads to substantial social, economic and health inequalities for people as they age.

People with negative views of aging are at a higher risk of mental health problems and illness.

Staying in good health reduces the cost of longevity to ourselves and society.

Agism is partly driven by a fear of growing old and an inability to contemplate death.

Agism is a belief system, and beliefs can change.

CHAPTER 5
WHAT IS AGING?

Imagine a child asks you: "Why do we get old?" Most of us would struggle to answer with more than: "Just because." And that's a perfectly valid answer because not even expert researchers in the field are entirely sure why and how we age.

A common scientific definition for aging is that it is the **"time-dependent functional decline that affects most living organisms."**

Therefore, it is not the passing of the years, but the deterioration that accompanies it as our hair turns gray, our eyesight weakens, and our knees creak.

THEORIES OF AGING

What causes this functional decline of our bodies? Of course, that is the proverbial $64 million question, and if we knew the answer, we'd all be rich. Scientific arguments about the causes of aging have been raging for centuries, dating back to the ancient philosophers who thought we aged and died so the old could make way for the young and life renewed. This theory continued well into modern times, but today theories of aging fall in two main schools, with many of them overlapping:

- Aging is a programmed process because living too long produces an evolutionary disadvantage.
- The damage concept, which says that it is the accumulation of cellular damage that causes aging.

THE HALLMARKS OF AGING

In the absence of one unified theory of aging, about a decade ago scientists developed a consensus model that identified nine hallmarks of aging,[1] with each hallmark having the following criteria:

- It should manifest during normal aging.
- Replicating it in the lab should have the same effect as if it happened naturally.
- Its reversal should slow the normal aging process and increase healthy lifespan.

In the upcoming chapters, I am going to take you through to take a deep dive into the hallmarks, for those interested in the science. If you want to an overview, each chapter has a summary and leads you to the recommended life strategy for each hallmark. Although I hope you do take time to read through the science as it is a fascinating area of research that is uncovering more about the incredible biological machine that is the human body.

The hallmarks are:

1. Genomic instability
2. Telomere attrition
3. Epigenetic alterations
4. Loss of proteostasis
5. Deregulated nutrient sensing
6. Mitochondrial dysfunction
7. Cellular senescence
8. Stem cell exhaustion
9. Altered intercellular communication

A major challenge for researchers in the aging field is understanding how the hallmarks interconnect, and how each one contributes to the aging process. Our bodies are complex biological machines and as changes in one system has the potential to change another, much of aging research seeks to discover how the hallmarks interact with each other, either positively or negatively.

However, before we begin, as so much of aging happens at the cellular and intracellular level, we are going to take a quick trip back to high school biology class to give you an overview of our cells and the fundamental role that DNA and gene expression plays in the aging process.

DNA—The Building Blocks of Life

Pause for a moment and consider yourself–your hands, your feet, your body–and marvel that a human being comprises between 30 to 40 trillion cells that make up more than 200 types of tissue, each with a specialized function like red blood cells (which are the most common), neurons, skin cells, and so on.[2]

Inside each of these cells is a nucleus containing the human genome–the blueprint of about 25,000 genes wrapped in 23 chromosomes, made up of **DNA (deoxyribonucleic acid)**, that contains the code to create and maintain our bodies. This genetic code contains all the instructions to ensure our cells are accurately replicated to safeguard our ongoing survival. Without this, we would soon fall into a state of disrepair and illness.

DNA *Structure*

DNA is made up of four nitrogen-containing molecules, called bases:

A - adenine, C - cytosine, G - guanine, and T- thymine.

These bases link together to form base-pairs in specific pairings:

A pairs with T, C pairs with G, T pairs with A, G pairs with C

DNA Base Pairs

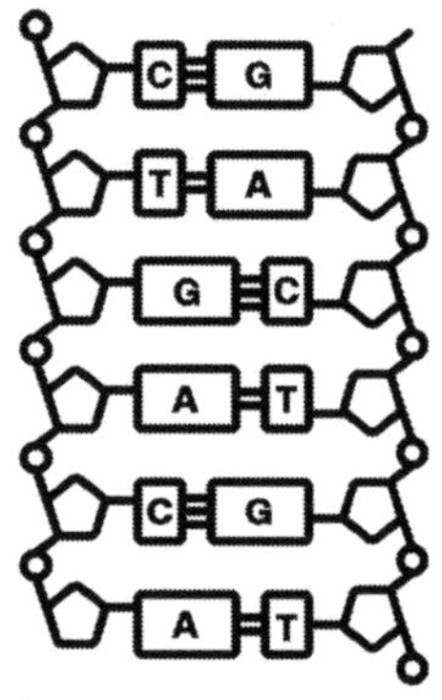

Each base is also attached to a sugar phosphate backbone. Together, a base, sugar, and phosphate are called a **nucleotide**, and these are arranged in two long strands that form a spiral called a double helix.

DNA Double Helix

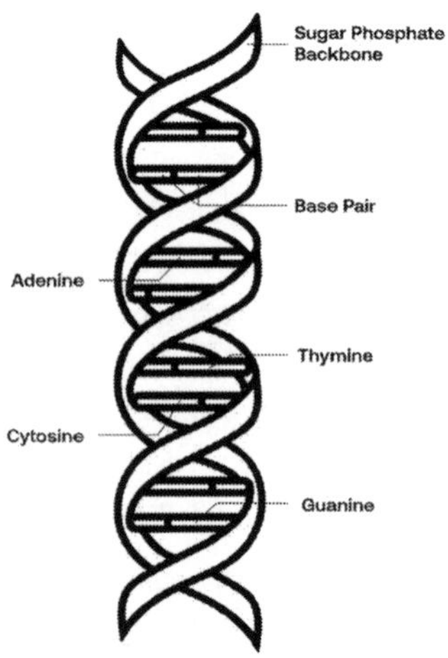

One way to visualize the DNA helix is as a twisted zip. The four bases of DNA are the teeth on the zip and link to each other chemically to hold the zip together. The fabric strips that the teeth are stitched to are the DNA backbone.

If one of the teeth is an A base, it can only link up with a T base on the opposite strand. Similarly, if there is a G base on one strand, it can only link up with a C on the other one. Think of Lego blocks joined together, but red can only go with yellow, and blue can only go with green.

This is known as the **base-pairing principle** and is fundamental to ensuring our DNA is copied accurately.

The Human Genome

Every cell in our body contains a full copy of this genetic code–**about six billion base-pairs of DNA**. This sequence is called the **Human Genome**, and we inherit half from each of our parents.

The Human Genome contains all the necessary DNA combinations used to create the proteins that do the functional work of the body. One way to imagine this is if all the recipe books ever printed were laid end to end, one ingredient at a time.

In the late 1990s, the **Human Genome Project**[1] was launched to map all the genes that make up the human genome. By the time it was completed in 2004, the project had mapped about 25,000 protein-coding genes, that is, groups of genes that when copied create proteins from amino acids.

Our DNA also contains non-coding DNA, which researchers are still studying to better understand its purpose.

---

1 https://www.genome.gov/human-genome-project

If our DNA code is the recipe, then **messenger RNA (mRNA)** is the cook. Think of a digital photo that you took of your cat that is so good that you don't want to lose it, so you make a copy and save it on your hard drive. However, it's a bit dark, so you lighten the copy, add some contrast, and boost the color. In our cells, mRNA is the software reading the original file and making the changes.

On the simplest level, mRNA reads our genes. Specialized proteins open up the DNA strand, then mRNA matches the bases using the base-pairing principle to create a copy but made of mRNA instead.

Once this is done, along come molecular machines, called **ribosomes**, that read the copied base pairs and assemble amino acids into chains to form proteins. Once the protein is assembled, it then folds itself into a distinctive shape.

YouTube has some incredible 3-D animations of this process, and I highly recommend watching them to understand these incredible molecular machines at work in our bodies.

The copying mechanism is incredibly complex to ensure our cells are accurately replicated. This means our cells have multiple mechanisms to store, protect and repair our DNA.

Protecting Our DNA

For instance, DNA strands don't float wildly around our cells, if they did, they would be about two meters long and tangle easily like thread. It is astounding that a two-meter (about 3 feet) chain of DNA is contained in every cell and a strand averages only about two nanometers (or two billionths of a meter) in width. That is about 40,000 times thinner than a strand of human hair.

To fit inside our cells, the DNA chain is tightly wound around specialized proteins called **histones**, like thread on a spool. Then it is wound up tighter and stored in **chromosomes** within the nucleus of the cell.

Chromosomes

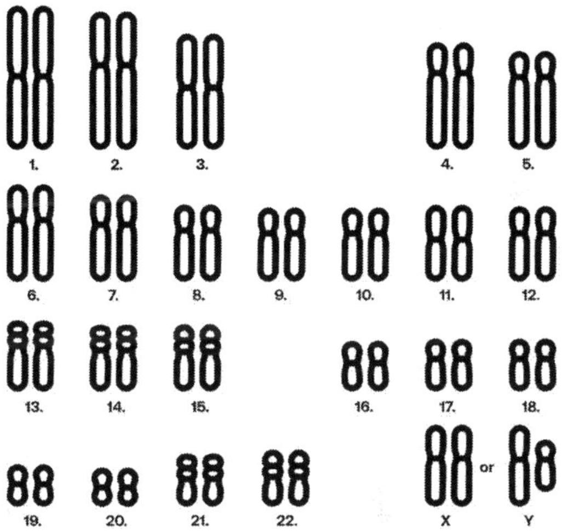

Humans have 23 pairs of chromosomes, 46 in total with 22 the same in males and females, while the 23rd has two copies of a XX chromosome for females and X and Y chromosome for males.

Our DNA Repair Machinery

Clearly then, safeguarding accurate cell replication is a major task for our cellular machinery, so alongside cell replication runs our **DNA repair machinery**, which fixes the damage from a daily onslaught of external insults such as too much sun, smoking, pollution, and stress. As we will see in the next chapter, accurate DNA copying and genomic stability is so critical to our survival that all organisms devote considerable time and energy to DNA repair, with our cells containing multiple mechanisms to detect and repair DNA damage.

These mechanisms are highly efficient, but mistakes (**mutations**) are sometimes made—such as a base missed out or the wrong one inserted. Usually this mistake is quickly repaired, or if the cell is too damaged, it is prevented from replicating or killed off. But if a cell mutation remains, it can alter how a cell functions, for better or for worse.

Although cell mutations can damage our cells, they also drive the evolutionary process, which is how populations change over generations. For example, blue eye color was caused by a mutation in one individual about 6000 years ago. Prior to that, humans only had brown eyes.[2]

A gene mutation is a **permanent alteration** in the DNA sequence and can modify anything from a single DNA base pair to a large segment of a chromosome that includes multiple genes.

Hereditary mutations are inherited from a parent and are present in virtually every cell throughout a person's life.

Acquired (or somatic) mutations occur during a person's life and are present only in certain cells, not in every cell in the body. These changes can be caused by environmental factors such as ultraviolet radiation from the sun, or when an error is made when DNA copies itself during cell division.

Without functional DNA, there is no life, and anything that disrupts or damages our DNA has profound implications for our health. As we explore in the next chapter on Genomic Instability, the integrity of our DNA is also a major determinant of how well we age.

Summary

Aging is defined as a "time-dependent functional decline that affects most living organisms."

There are two main theories of aging: programmed decay and the damage concept.

Scientists identified nine hallmarks of aging:

1. Genomic instability
2. Telomere attrition
3. Epigenetic alterations
4. Loss of proteostasis
5. Deregulated nutrient sensing
6. Mitochondrial dysfunction
7. Cellular senescence
8. Stem cell exhaustion
9. Altered intercellular communication

DNA stability underpins the aging process, and we inherit half our DNA from each parent.

DNA contains the code necessary to make the proteins that run and maintain our bodies.

This code is read by messenger RNA (mRNA), then ribosomes assemble amino acids to make proteins.

DNA strands are wound around histones and stored in the 23 human chromosomes.

Our cells' DNA repair machinery maintains and repairs DNA damage.

DNA damage results in mutations, which can be harmless or harmful. Some mutations become permanent and get passed along to our offspring.

DNA stability is vital for good health.

Chapter 6

Hallmark One—Genomic Instability

DNA—The Source of Life

Virtually all life on Earth shares one thing; we live in an environment often hostile to our existence. We need oxygen to breathe, but too little or too much will kill us. Exposure to ultraviolet radiation from the sun burns our skin, we drown in water, and burn in fire. We have to live in a narrow band of air pressure and temperature to avoid dying from the cold or heat or having our lungs crushed.

If that wasn't enough, we create our own threats by eating unhealthy food, drinking too much alcohol, driving too fast, sometimes partaking liberally of cigarettes and other drugs, and indulging in generally foolhardy behavior. Considering all these factors, it's a miracle we survive at all.

Internally, our cells face challenges too, with DNA replication errors, damage to the chemical bonds that hold the DNA molecules together, and free radical damage[1] all potentially causing harmful changes in gene expression, inhibiting cell division, or triggering cell death and contributing to the aging process.

Maintaining the integrity of our DNA is vital to ensure that our mRNA codes, assembles and delivers the correct

---

1 Free radicals are free roaming electrons that can damage our cells and are discussed in depth in Chapter 11 – Mitochondrial Dysfunction

proteins to our cells so they function properly. The survival of all organisms depends on this interplay of DNA and proteins. DNA needs protein to replicate, while proteins need DNA to create more protein. It is a complex dance and mRNA is the bridge between the two.

It is no wonder then that in the face of this multitude of threats, organisms evolved a complex network of DNA repair mechanisms, equipping our cells with intricate and sophisticated systems that swoop in to repair DNA damage the moment it occurs.

Substantial evidence from animal and human studies show that failures in these repair systems contribute to the aging process and are also responsible for several human accelerated-aging diseases (which cause people to look older while they are still young).

As detrimental as they are, understanding the causes of these diseases has helped researchers to unravel how DNA damage causes aging. Werner's syndrome, for example, causes signs of aging, including wrinkles, gray hair and hair loss to appear in people in their 20s, and can also trigger the early development of various types of cancer and hardening of the arteries–all normally associated with advanced age.

Nuclear Lamins

Damage within the cell can also contribute to aging. Lamins are **architectural proteins** that line the inside of the cell nucleus membrane. They provide a platform for proteins and chromatin to bind to and stabilize the structure of the nucleus, like shoring up a wall with scaffolding.

Their role in aging was discovered when mutations in the proteins that make up lamins were found to cause progeria, an accelerated aging disease. This is a very rare genetic disease that causes children to age rapidly. They appear to be healthy at birth, then start to show signs of rapid aging in the first two years of their life.

This is because of a mutated protein called **progerin**. Because it doesn't properly integrate in the lamin (think of a squished Lego block) it weakens the structure of the nuclear membrane.

Progerin also increases the frequency of unrepaired **double-strand breaks**[2] in DNA following exposure to ionizing radiation.[1] Why this is important is that if small children are showing signs of aging due to a protein mutation, it means aging is not a result of time passing but of cellular dysfunction, and this means it could be reversed.

The Information Theory of Aging

That is what Australian biologist and professor of genetics David Sinclair, a leading researcher on aging and longevity mechanisms, believes underpins **The Information Theory of Aging.**

According to Sinclair, the detrimental effects of getting older are caused by an ancient genetic survival circuit that stop cells from replicating when their DNA is damaged. The cell's replication gene is silenced (that is, stopped from working) until the DNA is repaired and only then is cell division allowed to continue. This process ensures that cells are copied correctly.

Think of a photocopier that is slowly running out of toner, so each copy is getting more and more faded. Finally, someone slaps on an out-of-service sign until more toner is loaded and the copies are perfect again.

---

[2] As the name suggest, double strand breaks are when both strands of DNA disconnect.

Similarly, Sinclair likens our DNA code to a digital hard drive or a DVD where our genetic information is perfectly encoded and can be copied without changing the original.

Over time, however, the copies of our DNA code made via mRNA and other mechanisms degrade and get lost, much like the toner fading on a photocopier. If a person tries to read the faded original, they start making more mistakes. Imagine it is a recipe being copied and they substitute salt instead of sugar!

It's this epigenetic "noise" says Sinclair, that drives aging in the same way as a scratched DVD or a damaged hard drive can't read the original data and starts skipping or can't read it at all.

Proof of this theory, according to Sinclair, is that our DNA retains its original functionality when an organism is cloned. The newly cloned individual is free of signs of any signs of aging that it's donor may have had.[2]

If we can remove the scratches and polish up the DVD, we can age slower and have better health for longer.

When we are young, this polishing is done by our cellular DNA repair crew, consisting of seven SIRTUIN genes, and found in almost every cell in the body.

The SIRTUIN Genes—Our DNA Repair Crew

According to Sinclair, these SIRTUIN genes in humans are descendants of the ancient repair gene, but over time they have taken on many new roles.

He describes SIRTUINs as: "*The directors of a multifaceted disaster response corps sending out a variety of specialized emergency teams to address DNA stability,* DNA *repair, cell survivability, metabolism, and cell-to-cell communication.*

Most organisms carry forms of the SIRTUINs and mammals have seven:

Three of them, **SIRT1**, **SIRT6**, and **SIRT7**, are critical to the control of the epigenome[3] and DNA repair.

The others, **SIRT3**, **SIRT4**, and **SIRT5**, reside in the mitochondria, where they control energy metabolism.

SIRT2 sits in the cytoplasm, where it controls cell division and healthy egg production.

How SIRTUINs Work

To prevent the DNA strands becoming a tangled mess during cell division, they are wrapped around proteins called **histones**, creating a **nucleosome**. These are bound into bigger loops called chromatin, which are again looped and coiled to form **chromosomes**.

Chromatin

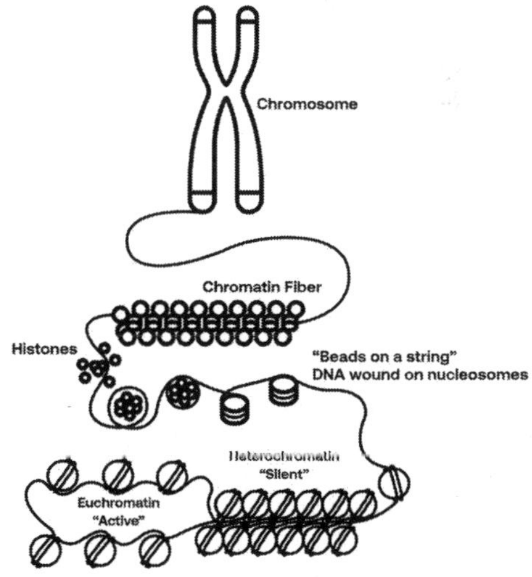

---

3 Our epigenome refers to the changes made to DNA that alter its function and is discussed in detail in Chapter 8.

SIRTUINs instruct the histone spooling proteins to tightly bind up DNA by removing chemical tags, while leaving others to wave around so they can be read, and proteins created. The chemical tags are called **methyls** and **acetyls**. In this way, some genes are turned on and others off. Accessible genes are said to be in **"euchromatin,"** while silenced genes are in **"heterochromatin."**

By removing these chemical tags, SIRTUINs help prevent **transcription factors**[4] from binding to genes and converting euchromatin into heterochromatin. In other words, they keep the DNA tightly wound up and inaccessible in the same way you can't see thread tightly wound up on a spool.

SIRTUINS Stabilize Human DNA

Unfortunately, according to Sinclair, the **epigenomic noise** that causes aging is partly caused by the SIRTUINs failing to return to their correct function once they have finished repairing DNA damage, like a robot vacuum cleaner that gets stuck in a corner instead of heading back to the docking station to recharge.

Aging is aggravated by overworked epigenetic signalers (the SIRTUINs), rushing all over the place then sometimes returning to the wrong location in the cell and silencing the wrong genes.

"Cells lose their identity and malfunction. Chaos ensues. The chaos materializes as aging. This is the epigenetic noise that is at the heart of our unified theory."[3]

The role of the SIRTUIN genes in the aging process has made them the subject of intense research to see if

---

44 Transcription factors are proteins that help translate DNA into mRNA

boosting their activity helps slow the aging process and assist in DNA repair.

SIRTUINs are NAD dependent, meaning they need nicotinamide adenine dinucleotide, a form of Vitamin B to function. In Chapter 19, I discuss how we can effectively supplement NAD to improve SIRTUIN function.

What Causes DNA Damage?

Despite our bodies having these extensive DNA repair systems, they are not always successful and, over time, the accumulated DNA damage in our cells builds up an contributes to disease and aging.

Damage to our DNA has two main causes:

1. Internal processes, such as replication errors and damage caused by free radicals[5] produced during normal metabolic processes. Free radicals can generate as many as 50,000 DNA lesions per human cell per day.[4]
2. External substances including diet, UV and ionizing radiation (that is, x-rays) and environmental chemicals.

Fortunately, there are various ways we can bolster and support our DNA repair systems.

Gene Mutations

Protecting our DNA starts with our parents and even our grandparents. How they lived can affect the health of their children and grandchildren by creating permanent changes

---

5 Free radicals are molecules (usually oxygen) that have lost an electron and seek to replace it by binding to other molecules, often damaging them. See chapter 11 for an in-depth discussion.

to their DNA, which can be inherited by our offspring. We discuss this in detail in **Chapter 8**, but if you are planning to have children, taking care of your health, nutrition, and managing stress is vital.

We also pass along inherited gene mutations to our children and there are many known genes that can directly cause or increase the risk of disease.

Some examples include Huntington's disease, caused by a mutation in the HTT gene. It is a **dominant gene**, meaning that anyone who inherits it from a parent will eventually develop the disease. Thankfully, there is now genetic testing available for Huntington's, so those at risk can check if they are carriers of the mutation.

Other genes, for example, the ones that cause cystic fibrosis, are **recessive**, meaning both parents must carry the mutation and pass it on for the disease to develop in their children.

Even if we inherit a gene mutation, that doesn't always mean the associated disease will manifest. This is the case with the BRCA1/BRCA2 gene mutation.[5] People who carry this are at a much higher risk of developing breast, pancreatic, prostate, and ovarian cancer.

However, the interaction between genes and the external environment is a powerful force, and even if someone inherits a mutation, they may not develop the disease unless they are exposed to certain environmental stimulus. As the expression goes:

"Genes load the gun, while environment pulls the trigger."

Fortunately, as gene testing improves and becomes widely available, it has become easier to be tested before having children to determine if we are carriers of any detrimental mutations.

Mutations like these differ from DNA damage as they are already hard coded in our genome and can be passed along to our children. Although damaged DNA can lead to mutations, if the damaged cells aren't repaired or purged, but it can also create permanent DNA changes that can be inherited by our offspring. Some, like the blue eye mutation, are harmless, while others like Huntington's disease cause immense damage. This is why protecting our DNA is critical to our health.

Substances That Directly Damage DNA

DNA is often damaged because of spontaneous errors during cell division, but there are numerous environmental substances that can directly damage it. Anything considered carcinogenic (cancer-causing) is also mutagenic (causes DNA mutations) and associated with various forms of DNA damage. These agents either directly cause DNA damage or link with other chemicals in our bodies that, when combined, become harmful.[6]

Fortunately, we can do a lot to protect our DNA as we grow, and even repair it as we age. In Part Two, I discuss what you can do to keep your DNA healthy while young and how to boost our DNA repair mechanisms as we age.

SUMMARY

Maintaining the integrity of our DNA is vital to ensure that our mRNA codes, assembles and delivers the correct proteins to our cells for them to function.

Organisms evolved a complex network of DNA repair mechanisms, equipping our cells with intricate and sophisticated systems.

DNA damage contributes to the aging process.

Accelerated aging syndromes caused by mutated proteins help scientists understand the aging process.

The **Information Theory of Aging** attributes aging to epigenetic noise that cause DNA damage. Repairing the noise could help slow or stop aging.

SIRTUIN genes are our DNA repair crew and if they become dysfunctional our DNA is not repaired properly, and errors arise.

SIRTUINs help keep gene expression turned off or on.

DNA damage is caused by internal factors such as free radical damage, and external environmental factors including UV radiation, chemicals and diet.

DNA mutations can become permanent and passed along to our children.

CHAPTER 7

HALLMARK TWO—TELOMERE ATTRITION

TELOMERES—THE CELL'S TIMEKEEPER

Earlier, we saw that our DNA is bound up into 23 pairs of chromosomes. While the DNA contained within them code for proteins, telomeres are non-coding repeating sequences of DNA that sit on the ends of chromosomes, coated by a protective sheath of protein called **shelterin**.

The common analogy given for telomeres is that they resemble the ends of shoelaces that have a coating to protect them from fraying. Telomeres serve a similar function by protecting the end of our chromosomes from the DNA repair machinery.

Because chromosomes are so vital to an organism's well-being, when the DNA repair machinery in our cells detects a loose DNA end, it either acts swiftly to repair DNA breaks or initiates cell death.

Telomere research has become an area of intense interest since the discovery of their properties and importance in aging and disease. Their role in aging was a relatively recent discovery, largely due to biologist Elizabeth Blackburn, one of the leading researchers in this area, who won a Nobel prize for her work.[1]

Her work built on the discovery in 1961 by biologist Howard Hayflick that normal human cells only divide a certain number of times before they die. This is now called the **Hayflick limit** and is largely triggered by how long our telomeres are.[1]

Telomeres

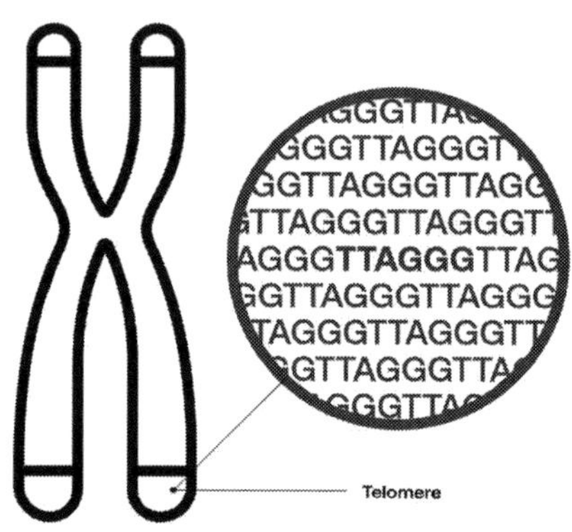

Telomeres are made up of only three base pairs: **TTAGGG**[2], repeated about 3000 times. When we are born, we have telomeres ranging in length from 8000 to 13000 base pairs, but by the time we reach 65, this is down to about 4,800 base pairs.

Telomeres role is to stop the end of chromosomes from being targeted by the DNA repair machinery, or from splicing onto another chromosome. It is thought chromosome 2 in humans might be the result of an ancient end-to-end fusion, which is why we have 23 pairs of chromosomes while chimpanzees, our closest relative, have 24 pairs.

---

1 https://www.nobelprize.org/prizes/medicine/2009/blackburn/biographical/
The Nobel Prize in Physiology or Medicine 2009 was awarded jointly to Elizabeth H. Blackburn, Carol W. Greider and Jack W. Szostak "for the discovery of how chromosomes are protected by telomeres and the enzyme telomerase."

2 A adenine, G - guanine, and T- thymine.

Telomere Attrition

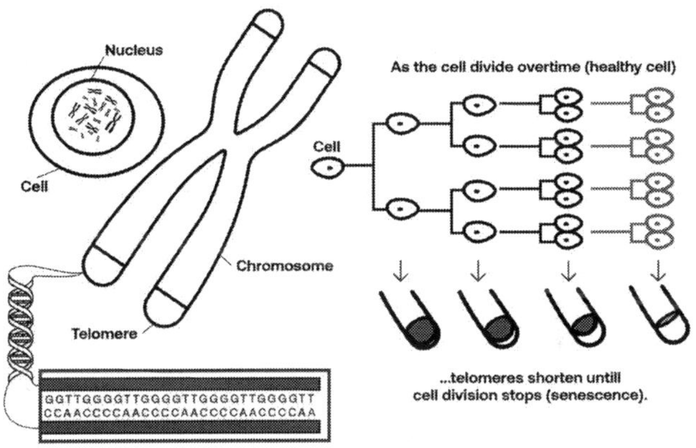

However, a side-effect is that telomere length affects our health and the rate at which we age. This is due to a quirk in the way cells divide. During cell division, the enzymes that copy DNA can't continue their duplication all the way to the end of a chromosome, so telomeres shorten slightly each time. In other words, the end is slightly snipped, so that every time a cell divides, it loses about 25 to 200 base pairs. It is due to this 'snipping' that once telomeres reach the **Hayflick limit** (about 60 divisions) our cells stop dividing due to the threat of the coding DNA becoming exposed and becoming at risk of damage.

Imagine you are holding a straw and you start snipping away at it. Eventually you will come to your thumb, and if you aren't careful, you will slice the top off it. Telomeres are the straw, in this case protecting our DNA.

Once our cells reach this limit, they enter a stage called **senescence**, which keeps the cell functioning, but prevents it from dividing. Cell senescence is also induced in response to damaged DNA to stop the cell replicating to prevent cancer. But when too many of a tissue's cells become senescent instead of renewing, it affects the ability of the tissue to function properly and then impacts our health.

This process happens constantly throughout our lives, and senescent cells normally destroy themselves or are removed by the immune system. Problems arise when too many senescent cells build up as we get older and start sending out **pro-inflammatory signals**, which damage the surrounding healthy cells. These signals are meant to tell the immune system to remove unhealthy cells and undertake repair, but they can have a detrimental effect if they continue for too long.

Cellular senescence and chronic inflammation are a major cause of disease and aging, and I discuss them in depth in Chapter 12.

Because of this continual process, telomere attrition is one of the primary mechanisms that determine how fast our cells age and die, and it turn, how fast we age.

Telomere Length

Telomere length varies widely as does the rate at which they shorten. Like many other aspects of our cells, this is strongly influenced by a complex interaction of biological, environmental, and behavioral factors. It seems that although we are bound by the Hayflick limit and, to a certain extent, our genes, we can influence the speed at which our telomeres shorten and take actions to stabilize them.

For example, it was found that skin that has had ongoing sun exposure suffer telomere attrition, whereas protected skin had virtually none. The effect on aging is easy to see when you compare the inside of your wrist to the skin on your arm. Wear your sunscreen![2]

This is an important finding because there is a strong correlation between telomere length and disease risk. People with shorter telomeres are at a higher risk of cardiovascular disease, early cognitive decline, and dying at a younger age.

A large study that measured telomere length across 100,000 subjects found that after controlling for multiple differences that might affect health and longevity, telomere length was a major predictor for mortality.[3]

As expected, telomere length tracks down as we age, but then seems to be higher in women and people over 75. This may not be because the telomeres have grown longer, but most likely because people who have longer telomeres to begin with have a better chance of living into their 80s and 90.[4]

Telomerase and Eternal Cells

It seems an unfortunate oversight that our molecular machinery does not restore telomeres as they shorten, but in some instances they can with an enzyme called **telomerase** that adds base pairs to the ends of our chromosomes.[5]

However, most cells do not express telomerase, and it is usually only found in cells that need to divide frequently, such as embryonic stem cells. If the telomeres kept hitting the Hayflick limit on these, then we couldn't create enough cells to develop in the womb.

In adults, telomerase is highly expressed in adult stem cells, male sperm cells, skin cells and immune system cells, that is, all the cell types that need to continually replenish and divide.

So why don't all cells have telomerase? Well, immortal cells aren't necessarily a good thing because endlessly dividing cells also fuel the growth of cancer. Research has shown that telomerase is hyperactive in 80 to 90 percent of cancers. This, combined with uncontrollable cell proliferation, is how cancer tumors form. This is why our dreams of immortality can't be solved by taking a hefty dose of telomerase, as artificially increasing it carries a high risk of triggering cancer.

Nevertheless. it does offer an exciting area of research for potential cancer treating through turning off telomerase activity. Researchers are investigating how it can be safely harnessed to reverse aging in humans without triggering cancer.[6]

When it comes to improving our health and slowing aging, there are safer strategies to reduce telomere shortening. Ongoing research has shown that telomere length can be maintained and shortening slowed with changes to our social and physical environment that support telomere health. Natural and safe renewal of telomerase is possible, and I discuss these options in Part Two.

Summary

Telomeres are non-coding repeating sequences of DNA that sit on the ends of our chromosomes to protect them from the DNA repair machinery.

Cells can only divide a certain number of times–this is called the Hayflick limit, and when a cell reaches the Hayflick limit, it becomes senescent.

Too many senescent cells in tissues can damage them and promote chronic inflammation and disease.

Telomerase is an enzyme that increases telomere length but can also support cancer.

Short telomeres are associated with a higher risk of developing chronic disease.

Telomeres can be lengthened with changes to our social and physical environment.

Chapter 8
Hallmark Three—Epigenetic Alterations

Our Genes Are Listening to Us

The nature or nurture argument of our growth has been raging for centuries, showing that humans have known for a long time that the way our lives play out isn't hardcoded in our genes and can be heavily influenced by our environment.

Yet a scientific understanding of how this mechanism works at a cellular level has only emerged over the past few decades. Today, the science of epigenetics (from epi meaning "outside of") seeks to understand how external influences can change our genetic coding. Epigenetics is the process by which two genetically identical individuals can differ in a measurable way.

This means that our DNA code remains unchanged, but our cells modify the way the genes are expressed. In other words, they decide what proteins get made by turning gene expression up and down, or on and off.

Epigenetic changes are said to occur when the outcome is different from the initial coding, such as when an identical twin is taller than the other one is. This is an example of an epigenetic change. Although their DNA is identical, something in their environment has either made one twin taller or the other one twin shorter.

Epigenetic Changes Drive Aging

Epigenetic change caused by the environment is one of the leading factors responsible for aging in humans. The clearest way to see this at work in humans is by comparing identical twins. They share the same DNA code at birth but often differ in subtle ways as they grow. (Epigenetic changes can even start in the womb). Scientists have conducted numerous twin studies through the decades to understand this process and measure the forces that shape individuals who are genetically identical. This makes twin studies invaluable as they are one of the few ways to study gene expression in humans over a lifespan.

Twin Studies

Due to the uniqueness of identical twins, twin registries have been created throughout the world. Because of ethical concerns about earlier studies, today researchers only follow twins raised in the same family environment as this provides a control for the genetic background and a shared environment in early life.

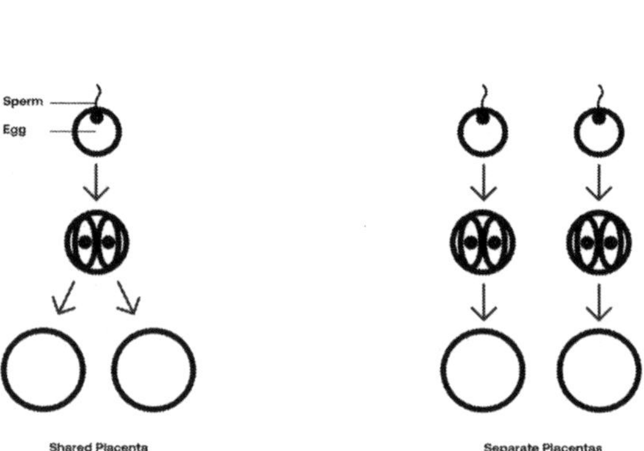

Other studies compare mono-zygotic (MZ) or identical twins with that of di-zygotic (DZ) or fraternal twins. MZ twins are derived from a single fertilized egg and share all their genetic material, whereas DZ twins are on average only 50 percent genetically identical.

By comparing how a trait shows itself in identical twins to how it is expressed in fraternal twins helps determine the chance that a trait is inherited and to what extent it is influenced by the environment. If identical twins have a higher chance (called the **concordance rate**) of sharing a trait then non-identical twins, then it means that trait is genetically driven.

For example, bipolar disorder was found to have a high concordance rate in identical twins. If one twin has the disorder, the other twin has a 38 to 43 percent chance of developing it, compared to 4.5 and 5.6 percent in non-identical twins.[1]

The longitudinal **Older Australian Twins Study (OATS)** follows more than 350 twin pairs over the age of 65 to investigate healthy brain aging. By comparing identical and non-identical twins, the researchers hope to understand which genes and lifestyle factors cause cognitive decline or cognitive resilience in later life.[2]

The ability to control for genetic factors means the results are more certain than if the researchers had studied a random sample of the general population, especially as the genetic risk of developing cognitive decline differs across people.

In one study, analysis of data from OATS and four other international twin studies found genetic factors account for only about 20 percent of the difference in changes to the size of the hippocampus in adults. The hippocampus plays important roles converting information from short-term memory to long-term memory, and in spatial memory that enables navigation.[3]

This means modifiable lifestyle and environmental factors play a major role in determining these changes. Exercise was found to be one important lifestyle factor that promoted the generation of new neurons and stimulated their migration to their proper place in the brain, particularly in the hippocampus.[4]

How Epigenetic Changes Occur

That epigenetic changes occur in our cells is clear when we consider that every human started as just one cell. Once an egg is fertilized, cell division begins, and nine months later we arrive at a fully developed human being with millions of specialized cells. Something happened along the way to create all those cells.

A germ cell is formed when a sperm fertilizes an egg, giving the new cell half the DNA from the father and half from the mother. Cell division starts and almost immediately specialization begins, a process called **differentiation**, which is how we get heart cells, skin cells, red blood cells and so on. What pushes each cell to change even though they all contain identical DNA? It is the activation of specific genes in each cell and this is the epigenetic system at work. It controls how DNA is used, sometimes for hundreds of cell division cycles, and the effects are inherited when cells divide.

Epigenetics at work

Earlier, we saw how the DNA strands in cells are wound around histones to stop them from tangling. But histones do more than provide structural support for DNA; they are active participants in making epigenetic changes, via long protruding tails that can be modified by **'histone tags'** which change the way a gene is expressed.

Our molecular machinery does this by adding a chemical group called **acetyl** onto one of the protruding tails. This alters the gene expression without changing the underlying gene sequence.

These modifications are known as the **histone code** and can cause gene expression to go up or down, but just how this works is still not fully understood.

DNA Methylation

Another form of epigenetic change is **DNA methylation**. In this case, a **methyl** chemical group is added to the DNA strand itself, but only to the **cytosine C** base. Again, the underlying base pair sequence isn't changed, yet the addition of a methyl group can dramatically affect how the genes are expressed.

When DNA is heavily **methylated**, it switches off gene expression and can even shut down entire regions of a chromosome. This is the mechanism our cells use to differentiate cells and ensure that a brain cell stays as a brain cell and a skin cell as a skin cell.

DNA methylation is a stable epigenetic change that is difficult to undo and often remains for life, whereas histone modifications are much more malleable and respond to all sort of stimuli from outside the cell, including hormones, addictive drugs, changes in diet and increased exercise.

Histone modifications and the histone code are the mechanism that allows the environment to interact with our genes and change the way they operate. If our cells decide there is an advantage to a gene being turned off by a histone modification, then this can lead to a permanent change through DNA methylation. This is how our cells adapt gene expression to changes in the environment, such as availability of nutrients or exposure to viruses, and these changes can become permanent and passed onto our children.

In a study of twins from when they were infants to later in life, the researchers found little difference in their DNA when they were young, but by the time they had reached their fifties, there was huge variation in the amount of DNA methylation and histone modification, especially in the twins that had lived apart for a long time.[5]

Chromatin Remodeling

We have seen how DNA is created in a strand, then wrapped around histones to form nucleosomes. The next stage is forming tightly packed bundles called **chromatin**, which helps protect the DNA strands from becoming tangled and protect their integrity during cell division.

Imagine a series of small beads that get wound around ping-pong balls, then get wound up further. As mentioned earlier, this packed-up form is called **heterochromatin**, but when the DNA sequence needs to be transcribed, it has to be unpacked again so the mRNA can access it–the **euchromatin form**.

As you may have gathered by now, our cells have a lot going on and the molecular machinery that runs our body is constantly packing, unpacking, and transcribing our DNA to create the proteins that keep us running. In many ways, our cells are like biological 3-D printers, but imagine the printer is constantly being blasted by radiation, oxidation and corrosion, and break downs.

This is what happens inside our cells, which is why we have such complex packaging and DNA repair systems to keep everything functioning. It's a bit like having a vigilant mechanic standing over that printer, ready to jump in and fix it every time it jams.

However, our DNA repair mechanisms are imperfect, so the amount of damaged DNA in our cells inevitably increases as we age, especially as chromatin modifications during DNA repair may never be fully restored to their pre-damaged state, causing progressive alterations in both chromatin-modification patterns and gene expression.

This is the 'epigenetic noise' that David Sinclair refers to Chapter 6.

This means previously silent regions of our DNA may become active, possibly disrupting normal gene expression. Meanwhile, other genes may become silenced near sites of DNA damage and, over time, disrupting the normal functioning of our cells and tissues.

Exercise and Epigenetic Changes

Our epigenome is highly dynamic and changes in response to biological factors such as development and aging processes, or external factors such as diet, stress and physical exercise. In fact, the benefits of exercise are largely driven through the epigenetic changes it causes in our bodies. Not only does exercise give us more energy, but it also plays an important role in disease prevention. Emerging evidence has found that exercise changes the epigenetic mechanisms associated with a variety of human diseases.[6]

Physical inactivity is among the top 10 risk factors for all diseases and is reported to be responsible for nine percent of all deaths worldwide, with serious health, economic, environmental, and social consequences.[7]

When we exercise, it induces biological stress in our bodies. It taxes our muscles and heart, and we burn energy in the form of ATP[1] to power our cells. Our body responds to regular exercise with muscle growth and, by increasing the number of mitochondria in our cells, improves our energy production.

Any changes like these in our bodies requires protein, and proteins are created through gene expression. This means the external environment (exercise) has acted as a trigger for a change in gene expression—an epigenetic change.

Exercise induces many beneficial epigenetic changes. It is already well-established that exercise causes muscle genes to adapt to increased load. It also activates glucose transport genes and mitochondrial genes, resulting in better glucose use and more energy production through cellular respiration.

Other studies have found that exercise up-regulates the methylation of proteins involved with inflammatory pathways and chronic inflammation. Up-regulates means increases, and when something is methylated, it is silenced, so by doing this, exercise helps reduce chronic inflammation in the body.

The effect of exercise to make epigenetic changes is remarkable. One study found that brief, acute exercise significantly altered the expression of 986 genes predominantly associated with cancer and cell communication in **natural killer (NK)** cells of 12 healthy men.[8]

---

1 ATP Adenosine triphosphate is the energy source for our cells and-is discussed in depth in Chapter 11.

Natural killer (NK) cells are unique innate immune cells that increase up to fivefold in circulating blood following brief exercise and are known to play a key role in the first-response defense against pathogens and cancer immunosurveillance.

What this tell us is that we are not powerless against the adverse impacts of lifestyle or biology. As the twin studies found, genes only account for 20 percent of the variability in our traits, the rest is a combination of lifestyle and environmental factors which we can change and influence to improve our long-term health and well-being.

Summary

Epigenetics is the process that causes two genetically identical individuals to differ in a measurable way.

Although the base DNA code remains unchanged, our cells modify the way the genes are expressed.

Epigenetic change caused by the environment is one of the leading factors responsible for aging in humans.

Identical twin studies are a way to study gene expression in humans over a lifespan.

Comparing identical and fraternal twins is a way to measure the amount of influence of the environment on gene expression.

The histone code using methyl and acetyl tags, and DNA methylation drive epigenetic changes, turning genes on or off.

Our epigenome changes in response to biological factors such as development and aging processes, or external factors such as diet, stress and physical exercise.

Exercise is a powerful driver of positive epigenetic changes.

Chapter 9
Hallmark Four—Loss Of Proteostasis

The Protein-Making Machine

Every level of our cellular machinery faces challenges that contribute to the aging process. In the earlier chapters, we saw how DNA mutations and transcription errors arising in our genome can worsen over time and hasten aging. Moving up a level, another mechanism that degenerates over time is protein regulation or proteostasis.

Proteins form the molecular machinery that run our bodies, yet they are made from only 20 different amino acids which, once combined, can create an astronomically high number of proteins. It is estimated that our genes can synthesize at least 30,000 different proteins and up to 6 million protein species.[1]

Protein Folding

Like the DNA repair machinery that works to ensure our DNA remains functioning, the **Proteostasis Network (PN)** works to safeguard the proteins we need to thrive through coordinated protein synthesis, repair, and degradation. To recap, our genes contain the DNA sequences that code for proteins, and these are transcribed or copied by mRNA. These copied sequences are used by ribosomes to assemble amino acids into the **polypeptide** chains that make up proteins. These chains look a bit like beads, and before they can be used by the body, they have to undergo a folding process to create a 3-dimensional structure–a sort-of cellular origami, if you like. This brings different amino acids together and places water-sensitive ones on the inside of the structure, away from the watery environment of the cell. Proteins also have binding sites on their surface specific for other molecules to fit into, much like a jigsaw puzzle.

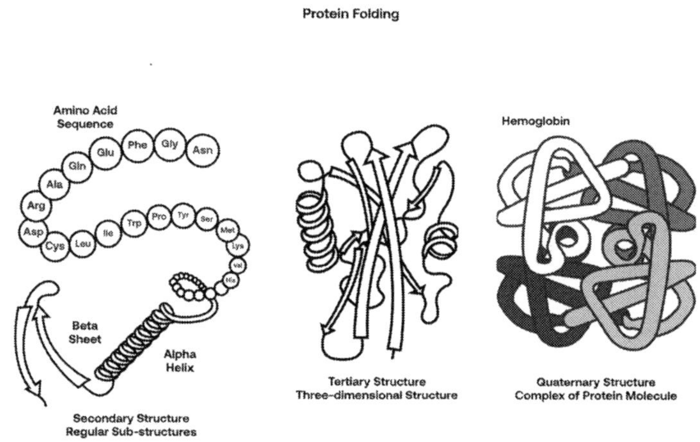

The correct folding of proteins is crucial because their shape dictates their function. This is why misfolded proteins can cause disease, because changing the shape of a protein changes its function. Unlike chemical reactions, proteins are literally molecular machines that run our body; they use energy, they spin, and they pump, so their structure determines the job they perform in our cells.

If you want to see protein machines in action, search YouTube for astounding 3-D animations of proteins at work. The complexity of some of these protein machines is staggering.

The folding process is normally controlled by proteins called **molecular chaperones**. Chaperone proteins also tag misfolded proteins for degradation.

As millions and millions of copies of each protein are made during our lifetimes, a random error in the folding process can result in a misfolded structure, causing the proteins to clump or accumulate together. Failure to fold into the correct structure usually produces inactive proteins, but sometimes misfolded proteins have a modified or toxic functionality. These toxic proteins can interact with the normal (or native) version of the same protein, causing them to also misfold, creating a self-sustaining loop leading to impaired function and cell death.[2]

This can worsen over time, with the accumulation of oxidative damage in cells, leading to the chaperone proteins becoming overwhelmed so that misfolded proteins and aggregated proteins accumulate in our cells instead of being cleared. The tipping point to cell death occurs when the replenishment of good proteins no longer keeps up with depletion from misfolding, aggregation, and damage.[3]

Protein misfolding is believed to be the primary cause of Alzheimer's disease, Parkinson's disease, Huntington's disease, Creutzfeldt-Jakob disease, cystic fibrosis, Gaucher's disease and many other degenerative and neurodegenerative disorders.

Alzheimer's Disease and Misfolded Proteins

The immense damage caused by misfolded proteins is evident in Alzheimer's disease (AD), the most common cause of dementia, and the fifth leading cause of death globally. Between 60 to 80 percent of people with dementia have

AD, and in 2016 the number of people living with dementia globally was estimated at about 43·8 million, more than doubling from 20.2 million in 1990.[4]

There is currently no effective treatment for AD, complicated by the fact that the disease cannot be clinically diagnosed until long after its onset when characteristic symptoms such as forgetfulness appear. By this time, the underlying brain damage is often advanced and irreversible.

However, there is hope of early diagnosis, with a recent study finding that in symptom-free individuals, the detection of misfolded amyloid-beta protein in the blood indicated a considerably higher risk of AD—up to 14 years before a clinical diagnosis can usually be made.[5]

There is growing evidence for several risk factors associated with dementia, meaning that lifestyle and other interventions might, if implemented effectively, contribute to delaying the onset and reduce the number of people who develop dementia.

Heat-Shock Proteins

Heat shock proteins (HSP) are a repair mechanism produced by our cells in response to stressful conditions to protect them from injuries. They were first thought to be produced only in response to increased temperature, but it is now known that they are expressed in response to several stressors, including cold, infection, and UV light.[6]

HSPs help stabilize new proteins and refold proteins damaged by cell stress. Researchers are investigating if up-regulating HSPs can help reduce or prevent the aggregation seen in Alzheimer's disease.[7]

The Protein Quality Control System

Like the DNA repair machinery, proteins have a quality control system to remove damaged and misfolded proteins, but this also declines with aging.

Autophagy

Autophagy is central to the quality control system as it removes damaged components, including misfolded proteins and recycles them to create new proteins.

When our cells are under stress, due to threats such as starvation and illness, the autophagy process is triggered so the cells can eliminate harmful material and get nutrients by recycling non-essential material.

In Chapter Ten: Hallmark Five—Deregulated Nutrient Sensing, I talk about how we can harness the vital role of autophagy and invoke it to repair our cells and improve how we age.

SUMMARY

The **Proteostasis Network (PN)** works to safeguard the proteins through coordinated protein synthesis, repair, and degradation.

Proteins are made from only 20 different amino acids, forming at least 30,000 different proteins and up to 6 million protein species.

Proteins are folded into 3-dimensional structures, with their shape determining function.

Misfolded proteins can cause disease, because changing the shape of a protein changes its function.

Chaperone proteins also tag misfolded proteins for degradation.

Protein misfolding is believed to be the primary cause of many degenerative diseases.

Heat shock proteins (HSP) are a repair mechanism produced by our cells in response to stressful conditions to protect them from injuries.

Autophagy is triggered when cells are under stress and eliminate harmful material and get nutrients by recycling non-essential material. It can be harnessed to repair our cells and improve how we age.

Chapter 10

Hallmark Five—Deregulated Nutrient Sensing

The Growth Longevity Trade-off

For millennia, humans lived in an environment where access to food was uncertain and our bodies constantly moved between being fed or hungry. This meant our cells evolved to quickly adjust to the availability of nutrients. This is essential for our survival because if we were only able to function when nutrients were readily available, as soon as the supply was cut off, we would shut down like a television when the power plug is pulled from the wall.

Fortunately, humans evolved backup systems that let us survive when nutrients are limited. When food is plentiful, we use glucose as fuel and store the excess as fat; when food is scarce, the body releases our fat stores and the liver converts them to ketones, which we can use as fuel. Switching to the fasting state, not only allows us to draw down and mobilize our fat stores, but it also gives our bodies an opportunity to repair and replenish resources.

The Role of Nutrient Sensing Systems

Nutrient sensing systems act like a vigilant mother, monitoring and activating the appropriate pathways depending on how much food we have eaten, and how much energy we are expending–sleeping, running, lazing on the sofa and so on. These systems also play a crucial role in our health and how well we age.

Their influence on aging was identified after a ground-breaking study, led by scientist Clive McCay in 1934, discovered that rats on a severely calorie restricted diet lived up to 33 percent longer than previously known Calorie restriction (CR) involves eating a well-balanced, nutrient-dense diet that reduces calorie intake by 20–40 percent without malnutrition.[1]

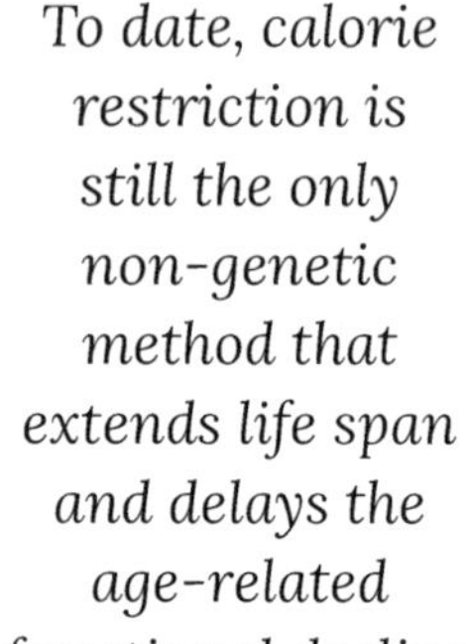

To date, calorie restriction is still the only non-genetic method that extends life span and delays the age-related functional decline in every species studied.

Over the next 80 years, similar experiments would be carried out on countless species, from yeast and worms to rodents and primates.

Nutrient sensors are central to this process and they run continually for our entire life; through the early phase of growth and development when our cells are building organs, muscle, and bone; into our crucial reproductive years; then followed by the years when we need more maintenance and repair.

The Importance of Homeostasis

Using cell signaling pathways, nutrient sensors process cues such as food intake and what is happening inside our cells to determine what is needed to keep them at optimal levels, a process called **metabolic homeostasis**.

We unknowingly respond to this process thousands of times a day. When we get hot, we sweat; when we get cold, we shiver; when our cellular fluid levels drop, we get thirsty. But when these regulatory systems get overwhelmed, it has disastrous consequences for our health.

Homeostasis requires the coordinated response of many different cell and tissue types. Unfortunately, aging results in a gradual deterioration of various cellular functions including metabolic regulation, causing a negative feedback loop–aging impairs the activity of key metabolic signaling pathways and the ensuing metabolic dysregulation results in accelerated aging.

Researchers believe that the age-related decline in metabolic homeostasis is a significant contributor to our overall aging. Studies in yeast, animals, and humans have found that several interventions–genetic and pharmacological–affecting the activity of metabolic pathways can also retard the rate at which we age.[2]

The Somatotropic Axis and Aging

Intense research has focused on several cell-signaling pathways that play an important role in aging and are heavily involved in metabolic regulation. Called the **somatotropic axis**, it comprises the **Insulin/IGF-1, mTOR and AMPK signaling pathways**.

We are going to take a deep dive into these pathways as they are central to the aging process, but be warned, it can get confusing! However, once you have an inkling of how they work, it reveals a great deal about why and how we age.

These pathways are deeply intertwined, coordinating the regulation and fine-tuning of cellular metabolic responses based on the energy available to our cells, nutrient availability, and what our hormones and growth factors are doing.

The most extensively studied of these is the **Insulin/ Insulin Growth Factor-1 Signaling (IIS)** pathway and the **mechanistic Target of Rapamycin (mTOR)** pathway, which between them regulate the life span and health span of most organisms.

They are some of the most highly conserved pathways in nature, meaning that they are found across a wide variety of organisms, sharing a common function and a biological origin from the earliest cells.

The Evolution of the Insulin Pathway

I am going to start with the insulin pathway as this is the one most people are familiar with. This system has its origins two billion years ago in the earliest multicellular organisms called **eukaryotes** that formed an alliance with bacterial mitochondria, allowing them to use the breakdown of carbohydrates to create Adenosine triphosphate (ATP)[3], the energy source of our cells.

Now, we take a big jump forward in time to four million years ago, where our hominid ancestor *Australopithecines* foraged on the African plains, largely on a seasonally variable diet composed of fruits, seeds, grasses, tubers, and some meat, most likely scavenged from carcasses. In this warm, moist environment, carbohydrates derived from fruit and berries were an important source of energy.[4]

However, it is thought that the amount of carbohydrate consumed by our ancestor was much less than today, from as little as a couple of teaspoons compared to high carbohydrate modern diets, where we eat the equivalent of a loaf of bread and more in a day.

As humans evolved over the next four million years, so did our brain size, tripling from approximately 400cm^3 in the earliest Australopithecines to 1300–1400cm^3 in modern humans.[35]

This process went in bursts, with periods of slow increases in brain size alternating with dramatic change. The first substantial jump in hominid brain size happened about two million years ago with the emergence of early members of our genus, *Homo*.

This happened alongside major changes in foraging patterns and consumption, causing a major adaptive shift in human evolution, leading to the emergence of *Homo Erectus* about 1.8 million years ago in East Africa, with a much larger brain and body size.

These changes occurred as the climate became drier, causing a decline in forested areas and an expansion of open woodlands and grasslands. This made animal prey more abundant and available, creating an attractive food resource. *H. erectus* was known to have actively hunted and was the first species to systematically make tools and use fire for cooking food.

Beyond the energy benefits, greater consumption of meat also provided increased levels of the **fatty acids** necessary for supporting this rapid hominid brain evolution.

Mammalian brain growth needs adequate amounts of two fatty acids: **docosahexaenoic acid (DHA)** and **eicosapentaenoic acid (EPA)**, which are the primary structural components of the human brain, and species with larger brains need more of both.

However, the evolution of a large brain comes at a high metabolic cost. The brain and other neural tissues have considerable energy demands–approximately 16 times that of skeletal muscle.

As a group, primates have brains that are approximately three times the size of brains of other mammals. But the human brain is some three times larger again than those of other primates, which means we use a substantial proportion of our energy resources on brain metabolism. The human brain accounts for about 20–25 percent of the resting metabolic rate in adults and 60 percent in infants, while it is only accounts for 7–8 percent in other primate species.[6]

This helps explain why gorillas who have muscles like, well. . . a gorilla, can get their energy needs from a diet of leaves and bark. Because of their smaller brain size, gorillas can subsist on foods that are abundant but low in quality, whereas humans need a substantially higher quality diet to meet the energy demands of our brains.

Moreover, it was not just an increase in brain size that drove our energy demands, but also an increase in brain cells, or neurons. The more neurons a brain has, the more energy needed to fuel it. It is thought that neurons in the human brain increased from 27-35 billion neurons in *Australopithecus* to 76-90 billion in Neanderthals, about the same amount as is found in modern humans.

Beyond the energy benefits, greater consumption of meat also provided increased levels of the fatty acids necessary for supporting this rapid hominid brain evolution.

In contrast to our large brains, humans are also relatively under-muscled (that is, we have less skeletal muscle) and fatter compared to other primates of similar size. The higher levels of fat in humans are apparent in babies. This, along with reduced muscle mass, means human infants can manage the growth of their large brains by having a ready supply of stored energy to feed it and by reducing the total energy demands of the rest of the body.

This is an important point to grasp as much of what our body does is largely energy management and conservation. Our brain and body manage the energy we take in through food to keep our body and brains active. Like a squirrel storing nuts for winter then hibernating, our body stores excess food away as fat to use later as fuel and seeks to conserve energy as much as possible. It takes from one system to give to another, ensuring important functions are maintained.

The Big Freeze

Over time, as humans migrated out of Africa and endured nine Ice Ages over 700,000 years, our diets evolved even more. Hunting and fishing became a dominant way of life, not just in high latitudes but also in warmer environments. We retain these dietary changes in our bodies today as genetically we differ little from our hunter-gatherer ancestors who lived 28,000 years ago.

Stone-Age People in a Modern World

To put this in context, it helps to understand why our genes have undergone limited evolution. We lived as hunter-gatherers for 84,000 generations, the Agricultural Revolution occurred 350 generations ago, and the Industrial Revolution, seven generations ago. Our genome simply hasn't had time to adapt to the world we now live in, which is why we experience so many health problems triggered by the modern environment.[7]

Our ancestors lived through the coldest of the Ice Ages on a high-protein diet. Their diets contained virtually no carbohydrate except the minor amounts found in the liver or gut contents of animals and in seasonal roots and berries. Other items which were gathered included nuts and shellfish, but these contain little or no carbohydrate.[8]

Because of this change from carbohydrates to high protein during the Ice Ages, our bodies had to adapt to the low carbohydrate intake because our brain and reproductive tissues still use glucose as their main source of fuel.

Briefly, when our body detects a rise on blood sugar (glucose), it releases insulin from the pancreas, which signals to our cells to allow the glucose in. Insulin also lowers blood glucose by increasing glucose uptake in muscle and fatty tissue.

But diets rich in protein also stimulate insulin secretion, accompanied by high glycogen turnover and stimulation of gluconeogenesis.[1]

We lived as hunter-gatherers for 84,000 generations, the Agricultural Revolution occurred 350 generations ago, and the Industrial Revolution, seven generations ago.

A consequence of a **low-carbohydrate, high-protein diet** is that it requires **insulin resistance** to maintain stable glucose levels, particularly during reproduction.[9]

It is thought that during the Ice Ages, those with greater inherent insulin resistance were able to redirect glucose from the mother's metabolism to the baby's metabolism, increasing the birth weight and improving the survival

---

1 **Gluconeogenesis** is the process of making new glucose from non-carbohydrate sources. This provides glucose when dietary intake is insufficient or absent.

of the baby. Essentially channeling glucose away from the mother to the baby.

Another study found that Native Americans, Mexicans, and Latin Americans, who have an up to 20 percent higher chance of developing Type 2 diabetes, may carry a gene mutation that entered our DNA through inter-breeding with Neanderthals.[10] The gene may have been advantageous for the Neanderthals in the low carbohydrate world, but is now detrimental in the modern world as it increases the risk of developing the disorder.

In other populations, factors such as geographic isolation or starvation may have helped those with greater insulin resistance survive and pass those epigenetic changes on to their children.

This concept, known as **selection pressure**, means that organisms that develop an advantage which helps them survive better, have a greater chance of passing that advantage off to their children. Thus, we evolved insulin resistance as a survival mechanism during the ice ages, but it has become a disadvantage in our current high carbohydrate environment.

The Agricultural Revolution

The advent of agriculture 12,000 years ago, saw increased cereal and starch consumption for the first time in human history. This may have decreased the selection pressure for insulin resistance first in Europeans, who have a lower prevalence of diabetes, even when overweight and obese.

Insulin resistance has also been proposed as a way our body copes with food scarcity. The **thrifty gene hypothesis** postulates that cycles of feast and famine increased selection pressure for a "quick insulin trigger" as a way to increase fat stores during food abundance, then for easy availability during food scarcity.[11]

An alternative hypothesis suggests that muscle insulin resistance was the key to survival during food scarcity because it conserved glucose by minimizing gluconeogenesis and preserving lean body mass.[12]

Yet both these hypotheses assume that there were famines before the advent of agriculture, but this is not supported by scientific literature. While hunter-gatherers would have had seasonal and geographical changes in food supply, severe food shortages or starvation were rare and more likely to occur after the transition to agriculture.

So, adapting to a low carbohydrate diet rather than the total amount of food eaten probably afforded the greatest reproductive and survival advantages for our ancestors.

The Industrial Revolution

The Industrial Revolution introduced the modern era of high consumption of carbohydrates. Prior to this, cereals were typically eaten whole, coarsely ground or flaked, so they were slowly digested and absorbed, eliciting a low glucose and insulin response, and a low Glycemic Index (GI) response.

But new high-speed steel roller mills introduced at the time, allowed cereal grains to be finely ground, and the fiber separated and removed. High-GI varieties of potatoes were also introduced to western diets contributing to a higher dietary glycemic load. This modern high-carbohydrate, high-GI diet leads to more insulin secretion, and therefore a higher insulin demand.

Nonetheless, even with these changes, it has only been in the past 30 years that insulin resistance, obesity, and

Type 2 diabetes has sky-rocketed in the human population, contributing to the rise of non-communicable diseases, shortening our health and life spans.

What is Insulin Resistance?

Because it is such a major problem for today's societies, I want to explain what insulin resistance is.

Firstly, food is broken down in our stomachs into three main components: **glucose**, **amino acids**, and **fatty acids**. These enter the bloodstream, and the glucose causes our blood sugar to rise. This signals the beta cells in our pancreas to release insulin, which in turn tells our cells to allow glucose inside so it can be broken down into ATP by the mitochondria.

If not all the glucose is needed, it is sent to fat cells and stored. However, if we eat too much sugar over an extended time, our cells can't cope and this causes them to trip, in much the same way an electrical fuse does when overloaded with electricity.

As our cells can't keep up with the over-supply of glucose, they become insulin resistant, that is, they stop responding to the insulin signal to take glucose into the cells.

This causes blood sugar to increase, signaling the pancreas to release more insulin to bring down blood sugar levels, creating a negative feedback loop.

Although insulin is vital for our survival, chronic insulin resistance is a primary cause of many non-communicable diseases and accelerated aging.

As the excess glucose is no longer being taken up by our muscles and other tissues, we become **hyperglycemic**, and the excess glucose is stored as fat, accelerating weight gain and leading to obesity.

Summary

Humans evolved in an environment of uncertain food supply and our cells evolved to quickly adjust to the availability of nutrients.

Nutrient sensing systems monitor our cells to maintain metabolic homeostasis to keep them functioning at optimal levels.

Age-related decline in metabolic homeostasis is a significant contributor to our overall aging.

The somatotropic axis comprising the Insulin/IGF-1, mTOR and AMPK signaling pathways are major metabolic regulators.

Humans first evolved to use glucose as fuel, but over the ice ages we adapted to a high protein/low carbohydrate diet. This led to insulin resistance as an evolutionary advantage.

Because of our large brains, humans need a nutrient rich diet, making energy management and conservation important biological functions.

The change to higher carbohydrate diets after the Agricultural revolution, and especially over the past 30 years has raised the risk of our inherent insulin resistance causing non-communicable diseases and accelerated aging.

Chapter 11

The Growth vs Longevity Trade-off

The **Disposable Soma Theory of Aging**, proposed by English biologist Thomas Kirkwood in 1977, theorized that aging is a trade-off by organisms between the resources they invest in reproduction and those invested in cellular repair and maintenance.

Because the amount of energy available to an animal during its lifespan is limited, for most species reproduction is given a higher priority, meaning it spends less energy on repair and maintenance, so the body gradually deteriorates once it is past the age of reproduction.[1]

The Importance of Signaling Pathways

One important signaling pathway where this focus on growth and development is apparent is the growth hormone (GH)/insulin-like growth factor-1 (IGF-1)/insulin system or **GH/IGF-1 pathway**.

As we saw in earlier chapters, the biological machines within our bodies are busy producing the proteins that keep us functioning and, like every factory, something needs to tell those proteins where to go and what to do.

All cells receive and respond to signals from their surroundings, usually via signal molecules that are secreted or expressed by one cell and then bound to a receptor expressed by other cells. This process integrates and coordinates the function of many cells. In other words, our cells talk to each other via a network.

This chatter is coordinated by **signaling pathways**, and these are important as research has found that therapies that target these pathways may offset age-related dysfunction and produce beneficial metabolic effects.[2]

Whereas the release of insulin is stimulated by **glucose**, the release of IGF-1 is stimulated mainly by **amino acids** broken down from proteins, and small amount of glucose.

IGF-1 is dependent on **growth hormone (GH)**, released by the pituitary gland in the brain in response to external stimuli such as sleep, stress, exercise, high levels of amino acids, and low glucose levels in the blood. This in turn stimulates the release of IGF-1.

Insulin-like growth factors are involved in the proliferation and function of nearly every cell, tissue and organ in the human body. Circulating IGF-1 stimulates growth in all our cells, from skeletal muscle and bone to organ tissue and vessel linings. However, due to the tightly controlled relationship between IGF-1 and GH, a deficiency or excess in either hormone can result in conditions such as dwarfism, pituitary gigantism, and acromegaly (abnormal enlargement in bones of the hands, arms, feet, legs, and head).

Production of IGF-1 remains high during our early years, peaking during puberty, a time with rapid cell proliferation and growth in height. By the time we reach our 30s, however, IGF-1 production drops off and declines steadily as we age.

It would make sense, then, that increasing IGF-1 could slow aging and indeed research on animal models found that altering the action of IGF-1 pathway in yeasts, worms, flies, and mice extended their lifespan. However, the results in humans have been conflicting, reflecting the complexity of the GH/ IGF-1 system.[3]

Growth hormone levels drop as we age, leading to a reduction in muscle mass and weight gain. This leads to a reduction in circulating levels of IGF-1. This is called the **somatopause**, as some of the symptoms of aging resemble symptoms of adult GH deficiency. Due to this, GH supplements were tried as anti-aging treatments.

A key study found that six months of GH treatment of men over 65 years of age, *who already had low levels of* IGF-1, increased muscle mass, bone mineral density and improved general well-being.[4]

However, later studies found that in *normal healthy elderly individuals*, GH only made small improvements in body composition and had undesirable side effects including joint pain and swelling, carpal tunnel syndrome, insulin resistance and possibly diabetes.[5]

To help unravel this pathway, researchers looked to a group of Ashkenazi Jewish centenarians who have two gene mutations on the **IGF-1 Receptor gene**[1] that suppresses IGF-1 signaling and decreases the transcription of target genes.[6] [2]

The centenarians who carried this mutation have a lower sensitivity to IGF-1, but higher levels of IGF-1 in their blood.

This is where it gets tricky, because high levels of IGF-1 are associated with an increased risk of developing many types of cancers, but also improved brain function, glucose tolerance and muscle and heart function.

---

1 **IGF-1 receptor** is a protein that is found on the surface of human cells and is activated by IGF-1

2 Transcription is reading DNA and making proteins, so the level of proteins made by these genes was deceased.

If it seems confusing, it is, so researchers then studied the offspring of the centenarians to try and figure out what was going on.[7] Although centenarians are considered an ideal human model to study longevity, they are also rare and often very frail. Their children are more numerous, and relatives of centenarians often have a higher probability of living longer and in good health than others.

The IGF-1 study of the offspring found they had lower circulating and total IGF-levels than other people of the same age and experienced fewer age-related diseases than the control group.

Earlier, we discussed how our nutrient sensing systems detect whether we are in a fed or fasted state, and signal to our cells to respond accordingly, either by hunkering down or driving growth.

When we go through growth, mostly when we are younger or reproducing, it requires plentiful resources, especially nutrients. Growth hormone and IGF-1 signal to our bodies that these resources are available.

A lack of growth hormone and IGF-1 when we are younger results in people who are shorter, because growth has been retarded. This was the case with the centenarians who had the IGF-1 gene mutation. They also tended to be shorter.

On the other hand, rapid cell division and growth is the main cause of cancer, so promoting growth can be dangerous, which is why most cells die after 60 or so divisions—the Hayflick limit mentioned earlier.

The answer lies in a trade-off between growth and longevity. Our body fuels growth when we are younger and in our reproductive years, then dials it down as we age to preserve resources and limit the risk of cancer.

However, when we keep our bodies in a constant state of over-feeding, because we no longer go into the fasted states that our bodies evolved to manage, we have fewer opportunities to repair or rejuvenate our cells. Instead, we end up on a constant growth treadmill.

The key to the longevity of the Ashkenazi Jewish centenarians is that they have better insulin sensitivity, so their cells are well-nourished, while the IGF-1 mutation slows their growth slightly. This means that their genetic makeup allows them use nutrients better and slows down growth, which slows cell division, leading to a longer life.

It seems the key to a long healthy life is a trade-off between sustained growth and slowed cell division—we need healthy growth when we are young but need to dial it down we age to preserve resources, give our cells time to repair, and limit the risk of cancer.

Insulin Resistance, Obesity and Type 2 Diabetes

This is why the detrimental effects of high blood sugar and insulin levels have become an area of intense focus due to the alarming rise in obesity[3] and Type 2 diabetes over the past forty years.

The worldwide prevalence of obesity has nearly tripled between 1975 and 2014, rising from 3.2 percent in 1975 to 10.8 percent in 2014 in men, and from 6.4 percent to 14.9 percent in women.

---

3 Overweight and obesity are defined as abnormal or excessive fat accumulation that may impair health.

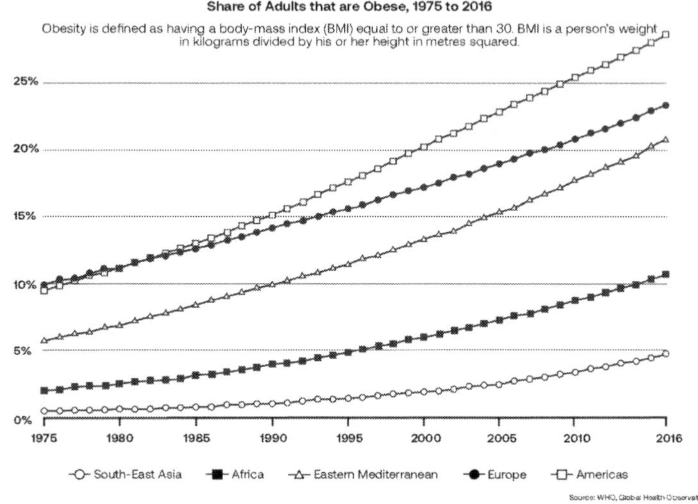

If these trends continue, by 2025 global obesity prevalence will reach 18 percent in men and surpass 21 percent in women, while severe obesity will surpass 6 percent in men and 9 percent in women.

This is equivalent to the world's population becoming on average more than 1.5 kg/3.3lbs heavier each decade. Being overweight or obese is linked to more deaths worldwide than being underweight. Globally there are more people who are obese than underweight, and this occurs in every region except parts of sub-Saharan Africa and Asia.[8]

Overall, about 13 percent of the world's adult population (11 percent of men and 15 percent of women) is considered obese, causing almost 3 million deaths each year.[9]

Being overweight or obese is also a major risk factor for two thirds of the leading causes of death from non-communicable diseases, including Type 1 and 2 diabetes, stroke, cardiovascular disease, lung disease, kidney disease, and liver disease.[10]

The damage this is causing us is devastating. Type 2 diabetes prevalence rates have soared worldwide over the past thirty years, and as low and middle-income countries adopt western dietary habits, their rates have also accelerated.

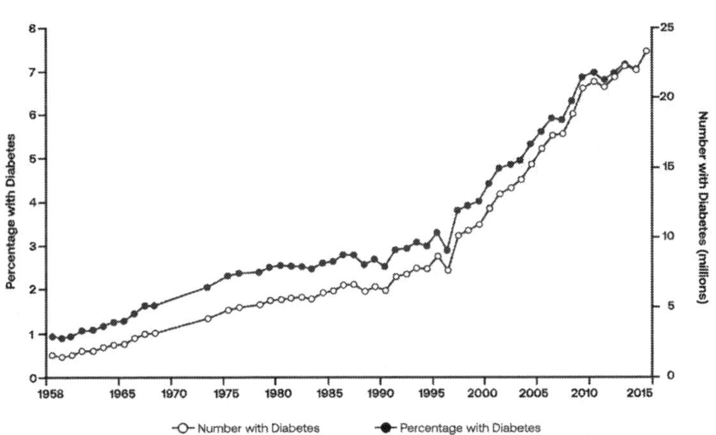

Source: CDC's Division of Diabetes Translation

According to the latest WHO estimates, 8.5 percent of people over 18 worldwide have diabetes and an estimated 1.6 million deaths were directly caused by diabetes, with another 2.2 million deaths yearly attributable to high blood glucose.

Type 2 diabetes causes a myriad of health issues, especially damage to the nerves and blood vessels, and can lead to organ failure, blindness, heart damage

Controlling our blood sugar and preventing insulin resistance is profoundly important, not just for preventing aging but also for our overall health.

and stroke, and it is now the leading cause of chronic kidney disease and liver failure.

Clogging the pipes-Advanced Glycation End Products

In the late 1970s, researchers began investigating the connection between diabetes and the complications it causes, such as heart attacks, kidney failure and blindness. They discovered that glucose in the blood bonds with hemoglobin by a process called non-enzymatic glycation.[11]

The more glucose there is in the blood, the more glycation that occurs, and the higher the levels of glycation, the higher the risk for complications caused by diabetes. This discovery led to the development of the **hemoglobin A1c test**, a simple diabetes diagnostic test.[12]

However, glycation has wider health implications as the researchers found that glucose also binds to other proteins and fats, changing them into pro-inflammatory proteins **called advanced glycated end products (AGEs).**

This is due to the "Maillard Reaction" something we are all very familiar with. In 1912, French chemist Louis-Camille Maillard described the changes that occur to specific proteins once they attach to a sugar during cooking, in particular, the browning compounds that give food its color, aroma and taste. You can see this clearly when baking cakes and biscuits or frying and grilling meat. These compounds are called **melanoidins**, and the same process occurs in our bodies, resulting in the formation of AGEs.

Exogenous glycation comes from foods we consume, while **endogenous glycation** forms within our body from high blood sugar binding with proteins and fats. Both contribute to the formation of harmful AGEs.

Although the body manages AGEs by flushing them out via the kidneys, long-lived molecules are especially vulnerable to glycation, especially if too many AGEs form because of high blood sugar or by consuming a sugar diet.

The formation of native AGEs is made worse in diabetes because of the high levels of glucose in the blood stream. Because AGEs are sticky, they cause molecules to stick together, a process called **cross-linking**.

Our body is reliant on the connective tissue that supports our organs including blood vessels, heart, tendons, skin, and lungs to be elastic and flexible. If they become bound by AGEs, they become rigid and harden, so instead of soft elastic they become like hard plastic. Over time, this causes effects like stiff joints, cataracts in our eyes, wrinkled skin, and hardening arteries, leading to arteriosclerosis. Think of a hose that has laid in the sun too long and begins to crack.

While short-lived glycated proteins have little effect, long-lived glycated proteins can lead to the formation of AGEs. These products are not easily eliminated from the body and play a significant role in promoting high blood sugar leading to insulin resistance.

Excess AGEs also oxidize blood lipids, or fats, causing them to be deposited inside our arteries and forming plaques that clog our blood vessels, raising our risk of strokes and heart attacks.

Glycation-induced biological products are associated with aging, neurodegenerative disorders, diabetes and its complications, atherosclerosis, renal failure, immunological changes, retinopathy, skin photoaging, osteoporosis, and the progression of some tumors.[13]

AGE Free Cooking

Unfortunately, the process that gives food its taste, color and aroma is the same process that creates AGEs, which is browning, or technically a high-dry heat technique such as grilling, roasting and frying. The higher the heat, and the longer the cooking time, the more AGEs are produced.

But a few simple measures can help reduce AGEs. Cook at a lower temperature with more moisture, so poached eggs instead of a fried egg, and slow-cooked meats rather than roasted. Other methods are stewing, steaming, and braising.

Marinating meats in an acidic liquid like lemon juice, vinegar, tomato juice, or wine can help prevent AGE formation by about 50 percent.

Foods high in animal protein and fats have the highest level of AGEs, so aim for a diet rich in plant foods and use low temperature and moist heat to reduce their formation in your food.

As with everything, it's about limiting exposure rather than removing it completely, so enjoy that barbequed steak but just a little less often.

SUMMARY

According to the Disposable Soma Theory of Aging, aging is a trade-off by between resources invested reproduction and those invested in cellular repair and maintenance.

The growth hormone (GH)/insulin-like growth factor-1 (IGF-1)/insulin system or GH/IGF-1 pathway manages these resources, co-ordinated by signaling pathways.

Interventions that target these pathways may offset age-related dysfunction and produce beneficial metabolic effects.

IGF-1 is dependent on **GH** and is involved in the proliferation and function of nearly every cell, tissue and organ in the human body.

Deficient or excess of IFG-1 and GH can cause growth dysfunction, but supplementing IGF-1 and GH have had beneficial and negative effect in humans.

Studies of centenarians who have an IGF-1 gene mutation in IGF-1 found a trade-off between sustained growth and slowed cell division, resulting in a longer life and health span.

Chapter 12
mTOR - The Master Switch

As I discussed earlier, for most of our evolutionary history, a scarcity of food was the norm rather than the overabundance of food many societies experience today, and our bodies are fine-tuned to manage both states.

One of the major regulators of our response is **the mechanistic Target of Rapamycin (mTOR) pathway.** This pathway anchors one of the central regulators of growth in the body and integrates nutrient availability, energy status and growth factor signaling to control of cell growth.

mTOR is a large **protein kinase**, which is an enzyme that modifies other proteins. This pathway senses the different nutrient levels in our bodies: the **fasting state** when we don't have enough nutrients, or the **fed state** when nutrients are plenty.

When life is good and food is abundant, mTOR drives cell growth by sensing amino acid availability and driving protein synthesis. When nutrients are scarce, however, mTOR inhibits cell division and initiates **autophagy** in our cells. This process recycles cellular 'junk'–misfolded or aggregate proteins and cellular components into healthy new cells, similar to scrap iron being reforged in a furnace to create new steel.

Understanding mTOR–Rapamycin

The discovery of a small molecule called **rapamycin** gave scientists and insight into the mTOR system. It was found in 1972 in a soil sample from the island of Rapa Nui or Easter island and research initially focused on its antifungal activities.

Initial studies showed rapamycin had multiple properties, including antibacterial activity, antifungal (anti-Candida), and immunosuppressive effects. In the late 1990s, further research found that rapamycin prolonged the life span of different organisms, including yeast, nematodes, fruit flies and mice, from 15 to 25 percent and also extended their health span. The mTOR and IIS pathways are also closely linked in the regulation of energy metabolism and glucose maintenance.

The finding that giving rapamycin later in life also extended the lifespan of mice was a significant breakthrough as it provided solid proof-of-principle that the pharmacological treatment of aging was possible.

The finding that giving rapamycin later in life also extended the lifespan of mice was a significant breakthrough as it provided solid proof-of-principle that the pharmacological treatment of aging was possible.

Inhibiting or activating mTOR affects how we age, but again it is a trade-off between growth and longevity. Inhibit mTOR for too long, and our immune system becomes suppressed and its effects harmful.

Yet, when we are overfed, mTOR stays stuck in growth mode, like an engine with the accelerator permanently jammed on. The goal is to find a balance between the two states that keep us nourished while giving our cells the opportunity and resources to repair and recharge.

AMPK—The Energy Sensor for Our Cells

The other two nutrient sensors, AMPK and SIRTUINS[1], act in the opposite direction to IIS and mTOR, in that they signal a lack of nutrients and catabolism instead of nutrient abundance and anabolism.

Anabolism requires energy to grow and build, while **catabolism** uses energy to break down. These metabolic processes work together in all living organisms to do things such as produce energy and repair cells.

AMP-activated protein kinase, or AMPK, is known as a master regulator of metabolism. It is an energy sensor for our cells and is activated when cells are running low on energy. In response, AMPK alters the activity of many other genes and proteins, helping keep cells alive and functioning even when they're low on fuel.

In the earlier section on insulin resistance, I talked about how glucose is the primary fuel for our bodies, but we don't use glucose in its original form. Once it is taken into the cell, it is broken down through a series of chemical processes (cellular respiration) in the mitochondria powering a process that creates a molecule called **adenosine triphosphate, or ATP**.

The more ATP that is present in the cell, the higher the cell's available energy supply. When ATP is broken down to

---

1 Refer to chapter 6 for more on the SIRTUINS

release energy for cellular work, a major end-product is **adenosine monophosphate, or AMP**.

AMPK *ensures our cells have the optimal amount of energy they need to function.*

AMPK is activated when ATP levels drop and AMP levels rise. Activated AMPK triggers the release of fatty acids from our fat stores and activates glucose transport, releasing additional energy for our cells from available or stored sources. AMPK also promotes autophagy (the recycling of damaged proteins), induces mitochondrial biogenesis, and promotes SIRT-1, which repairs DNA.[2]

Essentially, AMPK ensures our cells have the optimal amount of energy they need to function.

AMPK activation can be suppressed by inflammation, and when calorie intake is higher than we need to keep going, and more calories are consumed than burned, AMPK activation is decreased. With reduced AMPK activation, cells reduce their energy-releasing ATP-generating activities and shift to energy-storing processes, generating new fat deposits and creating excess new glucose molecules, in other words, making us fatter.

AMPK activity declines sharply with age. That is why we become less energetic and often gain weight as we age, while becoming increasingly vulnerable to cancer and diseases associated with impaired DNA and protein function.

However, AMPK activation can be restored through a combination of lifestyle, exercise, diet, and supplement interventions.

SUMMARY

The **mechanistic Target of Rapamycin (mTOR) pathway** is a central regulator of growth in the body and integrates nutrient availability, energy status and growth factor signaling to control cell growth.

mTOR mainly senses amino acid availability, and drives cell growth when nutrients are abundant, and inhibits cell division and initiates autophagy when they are low.

The drug rapamycin is a mTOR inhibitor shown to increase life span in organisms.

The AMPK nutrient sensor responds to a lack of nutrients and keep cells alive and functioning even when they are scarce.

AMPK is activated when ATP levels fall and AMP levels rise.

AMPK promotes autophagy, induces mitochondrial biogenesis, and promotes SIRT-1 to repairs DNA.

Chapter 13

Hallmark Six—Mitochondrial Dysfunction

Mitochondria—Our Cellular Power Plants

Mitochondria are tiny, microscopic organelles that live within our cells, and originated as bacteria that combined with early cells to use carbohydrate to create energy. They are not so much batteries as microscopic power stations and they generate the fuel our cells need to survive.

Mitochondria

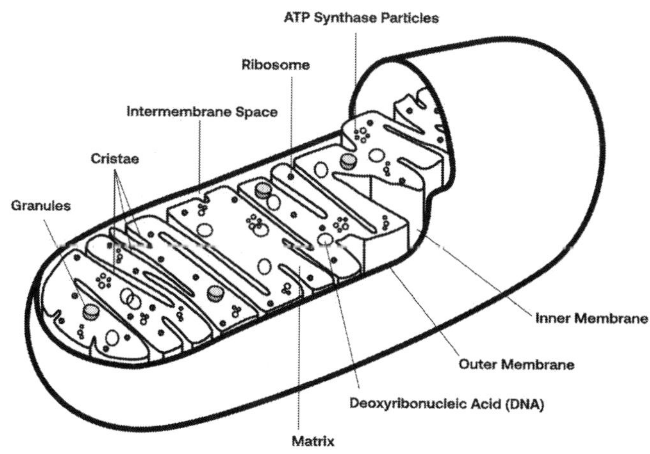

Unfortunately, mitochondria decline as we age, decreasing by about 10 percent every decade from our 30s onwards. It is partly why we don't recover from illness or injury as quickly as we get older.

Obviously, this decline has a detrimental effect on our cells and our health. Energy is key to cell health, and like a failing battery, lower energy levels reduce their performance.

Mitochondria are worthy of a book in themselves, and I highly recommend Nick Lane's "*Power, Sex and Suicide. Mitochondria and the Meaning of Life*" if you want to learn more about them.

Essentially, mitochondria convert glucose to a fuel that our cells can use called ATP via a complex multistage process that uses oxygen to convert the food we eat into usable energy to power our cells, via the Electron Transport Chain (ETC) or respiratory chain. Again, I recommend checking out YouTube for animations of this amazing process.

Breaking down glucose generates more energy weight for weight than the sun. In our 30s, we make our own body weight of ATP every day and this process is also responsible for most of the free radicals generated in our cells. Also called **Reactive Oxygen Species (ROS)**, they are a byproduct of electrons leaking from the respiratory chain in the mitochondria.

Free Radical Formation

We are surrounded by constant reminders to eat fruit and vegetables to protect us from free radicals, but many people would struggle to explain exactly what a free radical, so we are going to take another quick trip back to our high school chemistry class.

An atom has protons and neutrons in the nucleus and electrons spinning in an area called a shell around it. Protons are positively charged, and electrons negatively charged. If an atom loses electrons, it becomes a positively charged ion, if it gains electrons it becomes a negatively charged ion.

Simply, free radicals are molecules, usually oxygen, which have an unpaired electron in their outer shell. This makes them highly reactive, that is, they want to attach other molecules to stabilize their electrons. This in turn sets off a **chain reaction**. By grabbing an electron from another molecule or atom, the free radical will stabilize as it now has paired electrons, but the robbed molecule will seek to stabilize itself and steal another electron, and so on down a chain of molecules, which is why it is called a chain reaction.

This becomes a problem when free radicals steal electrons from biological molecules and damage them.

Antioxidants stop this reaction or damp it down by bonding with the reactive free radical. As the antioxidant is non-reactive, or poorly reactive, the chain reaction dies out.

Free Radical

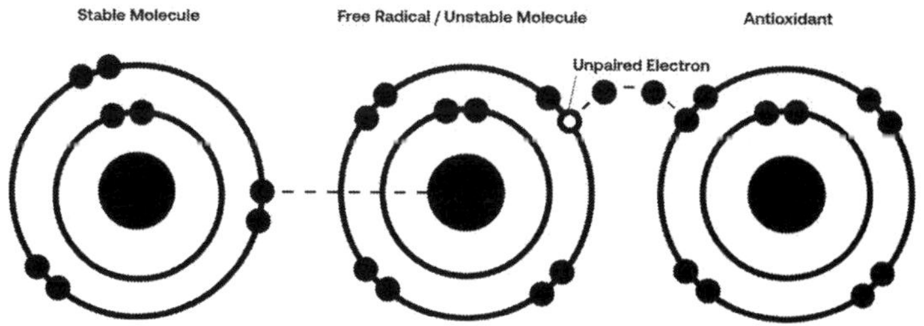

Part of the problem lies in the way cells break down food. Our cells have evolved mechanisms for breaking down glucose in small steps to convert it to ATP because breaking apart molecules releases energy. If it was done in one step, too much energy would be produced—an explosion as opposed to a contained fire. It is during this break-down process that a small percentage of electrons escape to form free radicals.

Rust, or iron oxide, is an example of free radical damage and oxidization. Given sufficient time, any iron mass exposed to air will eventually convert entirely to rust and disintegrate. Imagine that happening to your cells!

The Mitochondrial Free Radical Theory of Aging

The **mitochondrial free radical theory of aging** proposes that the decline in mitochondria function that occurs with aging causes increased production of these free radicals, which in turn causes further mitochondrial deterioration and global cellular damage.[1] Again, it creates a negative feedback loop.

To counter this, researchers theorized that if we supplemented our bodies with antioxidants like Vitamin A, C and E, we could repair the damage and hopefully live longer and healthier.

Unfortunately, despite a multi-billion-dollar supplements industry, this has not proven to be the case. In fact, in 2008, a Cochrane Review found that some antioxidants increased the risk of dying, particularly beta-carotene and vitamin E. Furthermore, a 2012 follow-up review found supplements containing beta-carotene and vitamin A increased rates of lung cancer in smokers.[2]

Another study of older men taking antioxidants and exercising showed that those who didn't take the antioxidants had better results than those who did.

It turns out that the body uses free radicals for certain tasks. One of these is a signaling mechanism within the cell. When the cell detects a specific level of free radicals, it acts as a signal that the cell is failing and induces it to kill itself – a process called **apoptosis**.

It turns out that free radicals play many roles, and we are learning more about them all the time. It seems paradoxical, that although free radicals can damage our cells, we also need a certain level of them to invoke cell responses. It's the Goldilocks rule: not too many, not too few.[3]

Further research has shown that antioxidant supplementation needs to be monitored in case it shuts down this important free radical cellular signaling that the cell needs to keep fit and healthy.

Unfortunately, although we need this oxidative stress to activate our cells' repair mechanisms, over time these hits build up, much like constantly repainting a damaged wall. Much of this stress is caused by the growing free radical leakage from damaged mitochondria. Combined with infections, this cumulative damage can lead to a chronic inflammatory response.

Again, it is a response that is echoed across all the Hallmarks, a repair system that helps when we are younger becomes detrimental as we age, often due to a negative feedback effect, and then contributes to other causes of aging such as inflammation

Another key to healthy aging is minimizing oxidative damage when we are young and repairing the effects as we age. In Part Two, I discuss ways we can improve mitochondrial function and reduce inflammation.

SUMMARY

Mitochondria are tiny, microscopic organelles that live within our cells, that originated when bacteria that combined with early cells and use carbohydrate to create energy.

They produce ATP, the energy source for our cells.

Mitochondria decline as we age, reducing our energy levels.

The process of creating ATP also produces free radicals, which leak into our cells. Free radicals are reactive molecules that have lost an electron.

Free radicals can damage our cells but also act as a signaling mechanisms.

Declining mitochondria function as we age causes increased production of these free radicals, causing further mitochondrial deterioration and global cellular damage.

Antioxidants can damp down free radicals, but also interfere with important signaling mechanisms.

Minimizing oxidative damage as we age reduces mitochondrial damage and chronic inflammation.

Chapter 14

Hallmark Seven— Cellular Senescence

When Cell Death Is A Good Thing

Life for every living being is a permanent struggle against internal and external stressors that can damage our cells. Fortunately for us, we have evolved repair mechanisms that strive to repair this damage as rapidly as it occurs, whether it is repairing DNA breaks, disposing of misfolded proteins or sending immune cells to fend off invading viruses and bacteria.

Without these repair mechanisms, our lives would be very short. One protective mechanism that our cells have is initiating cell death. This can take the form of **apoptosis**, which is programmed cell death; **autophagy** in which faulty cells are broken apart and recycled; and **senescence**, which is a form of cell arrest so that the cell still functions but can't divide. Cellular senescence is thought to have evolved as a means to prevent cancer cells developing, but even a 10 to 15 percent level of senescent cells in tissues is sufficient to cause dysfunction.[1]

Tissue renewal is essential for growing and maintaining our bodies, but it also brings with it the threat of cancer, which thrives on cell proliferation, especially as cell replication gives rise to DNA damage more readily than non-dividing cells. Within our bodies we have numerous types of cells performing different functions, and some can divide while others can not.

Examples of cells that can divide are the **epithelial cells** that make up our skin, fibroblast cells that make up the scaffolding of our organs, endothelial cells that line blood vessels and stem cells. These are termed **miotic cells** as all divide by mitosis (where a single cell divides into two identical daughter cells) so they can replenish our tissues. Other cells like the neurons in our brains and heart muscles cells don't divide or undergo senescence and are called post-miotic cells.

When a cell becomes senescent, it is still functionally and metabolically active, but can't divide and create new cells. Cells becomes senescent, for several reasons:

- Telomere-initiated cellular senescence triggered when telomeres become too short or dysfunctional
- Stress-induced senescence
- Oncogene-induced senescence triggered by cancer-causing gene mutations or the loss of tumor suppressor genes.[1]

This arrest process is stringent and there is no known way for a cell to restart the cell cycle once it becomes senescent, as it is maintained by at least two major tumor suppressor pathways, **p16** and **p53**, which are formidable barriers to the formation of cancer.

In addition to arrested growth, senescent cells undergo widespread changes in shape, gene organization and expression. Many also become resistant to apoptosis (induced cell death), which may explain why they build up in tissues as we age. Although it is not clear what determines whether a cell undergoes senescence or apoptosis, it may

---

1 An oncogene is a mutated gene that has the potential to cause cancer.

be determined by the nature and intensity of damage to the cell.

Once senescent, cells may shift towards **senescence-associated secretory phenotypes (SASPs)** and start to secrete substances which include interleukins, inflammatory cytokines, and growth factors to clear the senescent cells. These secreted factors are involved in a myriad of physiological functions including tissue repair and clearance of damaged cells, but also promote harmful effects, such as chronic inflammation or cancer progression, should the SASP persist.[2]

There are two main categories of senescence: **acute (transient)** and **chronic (persistent)** senescence.

Acute Senescence

Acute senescence is the part of normal biological processes and has a beneficial effect within tissues during embryonic development, wound healing and tissue repair.

For example, myofibroblasts are a differentiated cell type essential for wound healing. Because they promptly undergo senescence, this limits excessive scarring at the site of cell or tissue damage.

Acute senescent cells are eliminated through the activation of the SASP factors, which in turn activates immune clearance.

Chronic Senescence

Chronic senescence arises when there is a build-up of too many senescent cells in tissues. This affects the ability of neighboring cells to function well, compromising normal tissue and inducing cancer.

The senescent cell burden is naturally low in young people but increases with aging in several tissues, including fatty tissue, skeletal muscle, kidney, our immune system and skin. Aspects of the metabolic syndrome (prediabetes), including abdominal obesity, diabetes, hypertension, and atherosclerosis, are associated with increased senescent cell burden.

Senescent cell accumulation can also occur because of a variety of factors such as various age-related chronic diseases, oxidative stress, developmental factors, chronic infections (e.g., HIV), certain medications (chemotherapy or certain HIV protease inhibitors), and radiation exposure.

> *Cellular senescence is indicated in every pathological condition associated with aging.*

The Antagonistic Pleiotropy Theory of Aging

Understanding why cellular senescence can be both beneficial and detrimental may lie with the **antagonistic pleiotropy theory of aging**[3] which hypothesizes that genes or processes that are beneficial in young organisms, become harmful in older organisms. Although senescence protects us from cancer and DNA damaged cells when we are young, harmful effects come later in life as there is no selective pressure to eliminate the negative effects once we have passed our genes on to the next generation.

It seems harsh, but once we have reproduced, nature isn't that interested in us anymore!

This is the case with the **p53** gene that transcribes **tumor protein p53**, which acts as a tumor suppressor by regulating cell division and keeping cells from growing and dividing too fast, or in an uncontrolled way.

Known as the Guardian of the Genome for the role it plays in the nucleus, where it is essential for regulating DNA repair and cell division, it also initiates cell senescence when telomeres become too short. Although p53 is vital for cell health, more than half of all cancers contain a mutation in the p53 gene.[4]

In this instance, aging well is a trade-off between tumor suppression and accumulation of senescent cells. By suppressing cells and preventing them from becoming cancerous, our cells stay healthy, but too many senescent cells building up in our tissues ages them. Another key to healthy aging is keeping our tumor suppressant mechanisms active while clearing senescence tissue. I discuss ways to do this in Part Two.

Summary

Induced cell death is protective mechanism cells use when they are damaged.

There are three types of cell death: apoptosis, programmed cell death; autophagy in which faulty cells are broken apart and recycled; and senescence, which is a form of cell arrest.

Cellular senescence prevents cancer cells developing, but low levels of senescent cells in tissues is enough to cause dysfunction.

Tissue renewal is essential for growing and maintaining our bodies, but it carries the risk cancer, which thrives on cell proliferation.

The p16 and p53 tumor suppressor pathways act to prevent cancer forming.

Although p53 is vital for cell health, more than half of all cancers contain a mutation in the p53 gene.

Senescent cells become senescence-associated secretory phenotypes (SASPs) that can cause chronic inflammation if they persist.

Healthy aging requires a trade-off between tumor suppression and accumulation of senescent cells.

Inducing autophagy is one way to clear senescent cells.

Chapter 15
Hallmark Eight—Stem Cell Exhaustion

Healthy Cell Replenishment

What an incredible biological machine the human body is. From our DNA containing the code to build proteins that allow us to function, to the sensing pathways and mitochondria that monitor and provide the energy to keep us up and running, we are a marvel on two legs. Perhaps our greatest accomplishment is the ability to self-heal and replenish our tissues.

Every day, trillions of cells are turned over in our body. The average body makes about two to three million red blood cells alone every second, or about 200 billion red blood cells per day.[1]

Healthy cell renewal is one of the keys to a healthy life. Our cells are constantly replenishing our tissues and replace themselves every seven to ten years. Some turn over much faster, skin cells renew every eight days, epithelial tissues that line our organs renew every four to five days, while bone remodeling is a continual process as we grow.

How important is this process? Consider that without stem cells, we wouldn't last more than a few days as nothing would be replenished or repaired. If we cut ourselves, our wounds wouldn't heal, no new blood cells would form, or skin, hair or nails.

There are two main types of stem cells: embryonic and adult. Both can self-renew and to differentiate into specialized cell types. Embryonic stem cells form in early development during the blastocyst stage and are **pluripotent**, meaning they can form any cell type.

Adult stem cells arise after early development and have a more limited function. They can self-renew but are **multipotent**, meaning they can only form into one other cell type.

Adult stem cells sit dormant in our body until they are needed at which point they divide to produce a **progenitor cell**. These divide again to create more stem cells and new specialized cells to repair and replace the ones that are needed. Neighboring non-stem cells signal stem cells to divide when necessary, a task that the stem cell generally performs very slowly. In the skin, stem cells sit in a niche within the hair follicle bulge and give rise to all the cells making up our hair follicles and help produce new surface epithelial cells to heal our skin.

Senescence Stem Cells

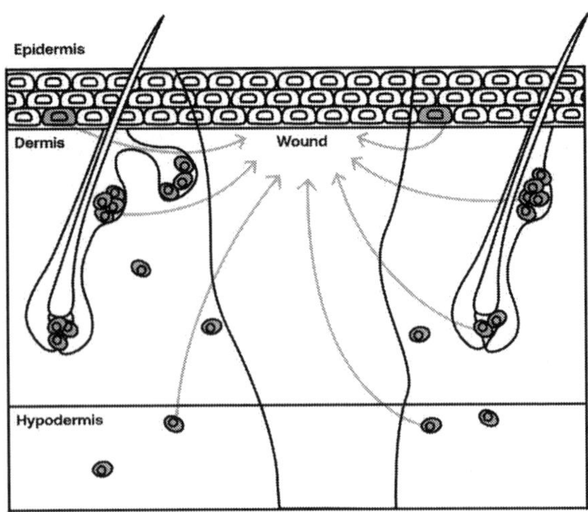

Stem cells sit quietly in a quiescent and low metabolic state to prevent exhaustion and to protect themselves from the accumulation of gene mutations that may lead to malignant transformation into cancer cells.[2]

Maintaining this state is vital to cell health as mutated stem cells that turn cancerous are incredibly dangerous. They can develop tumors from a single cell and are much harder to kill than normal cancer cells.

Fortunately for us, stem cells usually play a much more benevolent role. From the moment an egg and sperm join to create a fertilized egg, our stem cells kick into action to start building a human being. At first, they are called **totipotent**, meaning they can make any type of cell, but within a short time **cell differentiation** begins and cells become specialized. By the time we are born, stem cells have developed a new human from a single cell to an organism with thousands of cell types and trillions of cells.

This growth phase continues throughout childhood and adolescence, powered by adult stem cells creating new cells and renewing themselves.

Now the next phase begins as we head towards our 20s—keeping our bodies healthy and in good repair by replenishing cells that have reached the end of their life span and replacing cells in damaged tissue.

Whenever the immune system sounds the alarm, stem cells ramp up production, creating trillions of infection-fighting blood cells to fight off harmful invaders.

Unfortunately, like many other mechanisms in our body, stem cells in our tissues decline in both quality and quantity over time. As we get older, so to do our stem cells; we heal more slowly, and stem cell exhaustion may play a role in the development of some diseases.

How do we fight this? Studies have found that exercise may rejuvenate and increase stem cells in our muscles and brains.[3] As stem cells need a stimulus to become active and proliferate, researchers think that exercise can provide enough stimuli for stem cells to activate and get them mobilized–yet another reason to get off the sofa and start moving!

Fasting has also shown promising results for boosting stem cells, with studies finding risk factors and biomarkers for aging, diabetes, cardiovascular disease and cancer were lowered by fasting without major adverse effects.[4]

Stem cell therapies are a growing health intervention, but beyond the scope of this book, however I explore proven and safe mechanisms for supporting stem cell health in Part Two.

Summary

Healthy cell renewal is one of the keys to a healthy life.

Stem cells are essential to cell renewal. Adult stem cells sit dormant in our body until they are needed for tissue renewal.

Mutated stem cells that turn cancerous are incredibly dangerous as they are hard to kill.

Stem cells in our tissues decline in quality and quantity over time and play a role in disease development as tissues renewal slows.

Stem cells need a stimulus to rejuvenate. Exercise is one way to activate stem cell renewal.

Fasting also boosts stem cells.

Chapter 16
Hallmark Nine—Altered Intercellular Communication

The Invisible War Within

Without stem cells, we would never be created, but they march hand-in-hand with our immune system. Without its protection, we wouldn't survive more than a week in a world abundant with bacteria, microbes and fungi keen to inhabit our bodies as homes and use us for food.

How do we know that? Consider what happens to an organism once it dies and its immune system is no longer active. It is rapidly broken down and consumed by bacteria, and only a month after death, a body has already started to liquefy.

We are not alone on this planet–we share our world with trillions of microbes, invisible to the human eye but constantly surrounding us.

We even carry them within us, sharing our bodies with trillions of microorganisms that outnumber human cells by 10 to 1. Our skin is colonized by a diverse collection of microorganisms–including bacteria, fungi and viruses, mites. The mitochondria that power our cells were once free-floating bacteria, and our gut contains friendly bacteria that helps us to digest our food. Our DNA contains multiple stretches of non-coding retroviral DNA, inserted there by ancient viruses.

This bacterial genomic contribution is critical for human survival. Genes carried by bacteria in the gastrointestinal tract, for example, allow humans to digest foods and absorb nutrients that otherwise would be unavailable to us.

We evolved in an environment filled with opportunistic microbes and to survive we needed a system that could detect and where necessary fight these microscopic invaders for us.

Unfortunately for us, although microbes aren't living beings in the sense of having a consciousness, they are incredibly adaptive. As we evolved measures to protect ourselves from infection, they developed counter measures to overcome them, and to a large measure, microbes were winning. Up until 1900, the major causes of death were infectious diseases, such as influenza, tuberculosis and diphtheria.

The major advantage microbes have over us is that they can reproduce extremely rapidly, allowing them to quickly adapt to the protective measures of larger organisms. This is why we need an influenza vaccine each year as seasonal influenza viruses have been found to mutate more than 50 times a year.[2][1]

The human immune system is woven into every part of our body and cells and it is a hard-working machine. Unfortunately, aging tissues compromise or overload our immune system, causing it to malfunction, which in turn accelerates the aging process.

As before, we are going to give you a quick primer on the immune system, how it works, the role it plays in aging, and what measures we can take to keep it running well as long as possible.

---

1 As this is being written, the COVID-19 virus has already mutated a number of times, showing the speed of viral adaptation.

The Immune System—The Foot Soldiers of Our Health

It's hard not to be in awe of the molecular machinery that runs our bodies. Our immune system is an ancient system and for as long as there has been life on Earth, we have shared it with bacteria, viruses and parasites.

In the beginning, all life was just a single cell. Some cells evolved and became more complex, while others stayed as single cells, happy to live and reproduce in the bodies of the more complex beings.

As multi-cellular organisms evolved, so did the need for a defense system against these microbes. The **innate immune system** evolved first, and then the **adaptive immune system**. These two systems work together to form a coordinated response against attackers.

The innate immune system is a universal and ancient form of host defense against infection. It has developed over billions of years and is the first line of protection against attackers until our adaptive immune system kicks into gear.

The innate system has two mechanisms that responds to invaders—microbial pattern recognition of foreign invaders, and inflammation to fight off that invasion.

Because we have been battling microbes for billions of years, our cells have developed the ability to recognize the structural features foreign microbes. These are called pathogen-associated molecular patterns (PAMPS). We have receptors for these called pattern recognition receptors (PRR) and they respond to structures such as viral RNA, the proteins that coat viruses, yeast, and bacterial cell walls.

These defense proteins are encoded in our genes and passed along through the generations.

In humans, the PRRs are found mostly in white blood cells called neutrophils and we have dozens of these proteins that can kill bacteria, funguses, and protozoan parasites.

Some PRRs directly kill microbes, while others tag bacteria which are then eaten by **phagocytic cells**. A third category of PRRs called Toll-like receptors **(TLRs)** signal white blood cells that bacteria is present and instigate an inflammatory reaction. We are all familiar with the redness, heat, and swelling caused by an infection. This is caused by blood rushing to the affected site, accompanied by lymph fluid which causes the swelling and pain from increased pressure on the surrounding nerves. Although we mainly associate this with skin wounds, the same inflammatory response can happen anywhere in our body.

This response is largely carried out by dendritic cells and macrophages. Once activated, they release pro-inflammatory **cytokines** that trigger most of the inflammation. Cytokines are proteins that signal changes to other cells.

One cytokine, **prostaglandin**, signals nearby blood vessels to enlarge, which causes the reddening associated with inflammation.

The invading bacteria also activate a microbial-killing protein complex called **complement**, which attaches to antibodies and helps them kill infected cells.

Fragments of the complement system activate another cell type called mast cells, which release histamines. This results in blood vessels becoming leaky, allowing white blood cells to leave the bloodstream and head to the site of the infection.

Other cytokines are released to attract the white blood cells to the infection. All these cells arriving at the infection site cause swelling.

Meanwhile, more cytokines activate our pain receptors to let the brain know trouble is afoot or go directly to the brain and trigger a rise in body temperature to help kill off the bacteria.

This happens immediately to attack bacteria until our adaptive immune system kicks into gear, which can take two to three days. It then comes with specific antibodies created for that particular pathogen.

This first response is called **acute inflammation** and usually once the infection is overcome, inflammation and swelling reduces.

Inflammaging

Inflammation is effective as an acute response to disease, but it can be deadly although it has protected us against microbes for billions of years.

Unfortunately, as we get older, the inflammation response can become chronic—a process known as inflammaging— in which we experience a constant level of inflammation within our bodies that aggravates our tissues and accelerates the aging process.

When an acute infection resolves and inflammation disappears, it usually does no harm to our tissues. As we age, however, the build-up of senescent cells secreting pro-inflammatory cytokines, the failure of the immune system to clear pathogens and infected cells, and increased levels of free radicals constantly generate antigens that stimulate the immune system, causing low grade inflammation. Another source of aggravation is microbiota leaking from the gut into the blood circulation of tissues.

Obesity and Inflammation

A large body of evidence has also found that obesity drives chronic inflammation. Being obese is a risk factor for many non-communicable diseases, but it's effect on the immune system also makes it a risk factor for infectious diseases.

High levels of fatty tissue can trigger inflammation and suppress the immune system. In animal studies, obese mice had a six-fold increased risk of dying from influenza.[3]

This chronic state of inflammation also interferes with insulin receptors and contributes to the development of type 2 diabetes. Elements of the immune system also sit in adipose (fatty) tissue, particularly macrophages. In lean individuals, this is about 10 percent but in obese individuals, macrophages can make up 40-50 percent of fatty tissue, again driving chronic inflammation.[4]

Chronic inflammation underpins many diseases of aging, and as we have seen, they are intertwined with numerous overlapping effects. For example, if we look back to the SIRTUIN genes in Hallmark 1, boosting SIRT-1 has been found to damp down inflammation-related genes, as does reducing free radical leakage.

Preventing and reducing chronic inflammation is one of the best ways to improve our health. It has a multi-system effect and is a major driver of aging. Fortunately, multiple ways to do this have been identified, which I will discuss ahead in part two.

Summary

Our immune system is an ancient mechanism that protects our body from foreign invaders.

We share our world with trillions of invisible microbes that constantly surround us and are incredibly adaptive.

The innate immune system is a universal and ancient form of host defense against infection and protects until the adaptive immune system can respond to invaders with antibodies.

Components of the innate immune system use inflammation to fight infections, these include phagocytic cells, cytokines, and complement.

The failure of the immune system to clear pathogens and infected cells can cause chronic inflammation.

Obesity can also drive chronic inflammation.

Chronic inflammation underpins many diseases of aging but activating SIRT-1 can help damp it down.

Bringing It Together

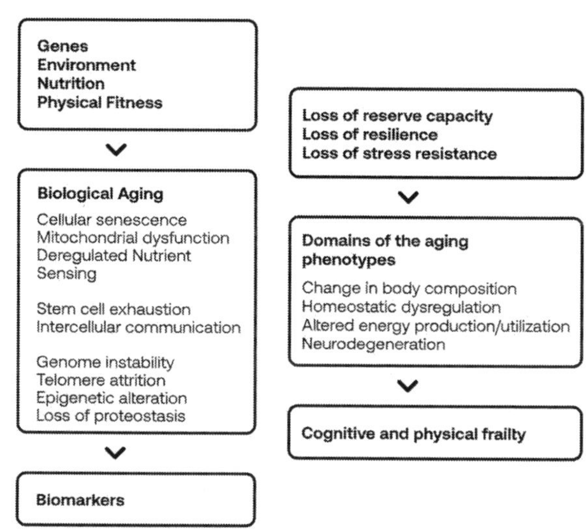

That's the end of our journey through the hallmarks, and I hope the one thing you take away is how deeply enmeshed they are. To make it easier to understand (even for researchers!), they have been grouped into three main categories: primary, antagonistic, and integrative.

The primary hallmarks, genomic instability, telomere attrition, epigenetic alteration, and loss of proteostasis are considered the initiating triggers, whose damaging consequences progressively accumulate with time.

The antagonistic hallmarks: deregulated nutrient sensing, mitochondrial dysfunction, and cellular senescence, are beneficial processes that become progressively harmful over time in a process that is partly promoted or accelerated by the primary hallmarks.

Finally, stem cell exhaustion and altered intercellular communication, the integrative hallmarks, are caused mainly by the accumulated damage from the primary and antagonistic hallmarks.

In other words, the effects of aging are global and intertwined, so interventions in one area has the potential to improve or sometimes worsen others.

In Part Two, I am going to offer strategies in line with the hallmarks to help you live a long healthy life, whatever age you are now.

PART TWO

I had to wait 110 years to become famous.
I intend to enjoy it as long as possible.

Jeanne Calment, the oldest recorded human, aged 120.

Chapter 17

It's Never Too Soon Or Too Late To Start

Travelling through the Hallmarks may seem daunting. There seems so much that can go wrong with us, is there any point in trying?

Fortunately for us, the answer is a solid yes because although health spans may have stalled overall globally, on an individual level many people are enjoying longer, healthier and happier lives.

It's important that we start working on how well we age sooner rather than later. In the not-too-distant future medical interventions and treatments will accelerate the length of time of our health span as well as our lifespan. The sooner you tune your cells up, the better placed you will be when these life and health extension technologies arrive.

But in a world saturated with images of youth, where we are bombarded with advertising and marketing trying to sell us products to maintain the illusion of youth, role models of successful aging can get lost in the noise, so I wanted to share an inspiring example with you.

A Role Model for Health Aging

American woman Ernestine Shepherd held a Guinness Book of Records title as the oldest competitive female bodybuilder when she was 79. *Today. Ernestine is no longer competing but is still an active, strong, and extremely fit 83-year-old, regularly posting on her Facebook page photos of her 20-mile walks or two-hour stationary cycling sessions.*

However, she didn't start that way. In her youth, she says she had little interest in athletics or exercise of any kind, and at age 56 described herself as "a sedentary, well-padded school secretary and slug" who had never worked out a day in her life, until she went swimsuit shopping with her sister Velvet. Somewhat dismayed at their appearance, they decided it was time to get fit, so they joined a gym and began working out. At first Ernestine wasn't as keen as her sister, but sadly, soon after, Velvet fell ill and died from a brain aneurysm.

Ernestine became depressed but she returned to the gym, determined to honor her sister's memory.

Often, when it comes to healthy long-lived people, there is a tendency to dismiss it with "Oh, they must have good genes," but Ernestine is a shining example of why it is never too late to start, and how small, incremental changes have a compounding effect. On her website Ernestine writes that she started slowly, building her body step-by-step under the guidance of a personal trainer, and ensuring that she had good nutrition.

If you want to see what is possible, check out Ernestine's website: ernestineshepherd.net and videos about her on YouTube.

Ernestine is an outstanding example that we have more control over how well we age than we often believe. She went from a sedentary 56-year-old to a vital, bodybuilding powerhouse, with no obvious genetic advantage.

Living a long vital healthy life is within our grasp, and it's easy to find other examples of people aging well like Ernestine in our daily lives: the 70-or 80-year-old striding past you on a daily walk, doing lengths at the local swimming pool, or practicing tai chi in the park. Unfortunately, our society is so geared towards chasing youth, that we ignore the achievements that people make across their entire life span.

Living Like the Blue Zones

So, how do we start the process of planning to live with health and vitality? We can begin with the special places on the planet where people have already increased their health spans– the Blue Zones. These regions were identified in a 2005 National Geographic magazine about places in the world where people seemed to live longer than average and had the highest percentage of centenarians: Loma Linda, CA, USA; Nicoya, Costa Rica; Sardinia, Italy; Ikaria, Greece; and Okinawa, Japan.

The areas were dubbed Blue Zones, and researchers identified nine lifestyle factors that they believe contribute to the inhabitants' longevity and slow the aging process.

Move naturally. Exercise is part of daily life. Blue Zone residents live in environments where they constantly move without thinking about it, such as growing gardens and not having mechanical conveniences for house and yard work.

Purpose. The Okinawans call it *Ikigai* and the Nicoyans call it *plan de vida*; for both, it translates to "why I wake up in the morning." Having a sense of purpose can give you up to seven years of extra life expectancy.

Downshift. Although people in the Blue Zones experience stress, they adopt routines to manage that stress. Okinawans take a few moments each day to remember their ancestors; Loma Linda Adventists pray; Ikarians take a nap; and Sardinians do happy hour.

80% Rule. *Hara hachi bu–Eat until you're 80 percent full.* The Okinawan 2500-year old Confucian mantra is said before meals reminds them to stop eating before they are full. People in the Blue Zones eat their smallest meal in the late afternoon or early evening, then do not eat any more the rest of the day.

Plant slant. Beans, including fava, black, soy, and lentils, are the cornerstone of most centenarian diets. Meat is eaten on average only five times per month. Serving sizes are small, about the size of a deck of cards.

Wine at 5. People in all Blue Zones (except the Seventh Day Adventists) drink alcohol moderately and regularly. The trick is to drink one or two glasses per day with friends and with food.

Belong. All but five of the 263 centenarians interviewed belonged to some faith-based community. Denomination does not seem to matter.

Loved ones first. People in the Blue Zones put their families first. This means keeping aging parents and grandparents nearby or in the home (it lowers disease and mortality rates of children in the home too). They commit to a life partner and invest in their children with time and love.

Right tribe. The world's longest-lived people chose – or were born into–social circles that support healthy behaviors. Okinawans create moais–groups of five friends that committed to each other for life.

Research from the Framingham Studies shows that smoking, obesity, happiness and even loneliness are contagious, so the social networks of long-lived people have favorably shaped their health behaviors.[1]

Chapter 18

It's In Their Genes

Despite these lifestyle factors, Dr Nir Barzilai, director of the Longevity Genes Project, an ongoing genetic study of more than 600 families of Ashkenazi Jewish centenarians and their children, believes that there is also a strong genetic component to explain the longevity of the Blue Zone inhabitants. He noted that in the Sardinian Blue Zone, nearby villages have the same environmental conditions, yet the inhabitants don't live as long.[1]

There is no denying that some genetic mutations do convey a longevity advantage for some population groups. For example, the two IGF-1 mutations in the Ashkenazi Jews that Dr Barzilai studies (see Chapter 11) and others found elsewhere in the world.[2]

In Japan, a mitochondrial gene variant, Mt5178A, found in 45 percent of Japanese, is related to longevity, with those having the variant 50 percent more likely to live to be 100 and in better health as they age. This mutation is rarely found in other population groups and may partly explain why the Japanese as a whole enjoy the highest life expectancy in the world.

Another mutation discovered in an Indiana Amish community helps the carriers live 10 percent longer than average. Researchers first became interested in this community because they suffered a higher than average incidence of a rare bleeding disorder caused by a mutation on the SERPINE1 gene.[3]

This mutation prevents the regulation of a protein called PAI-1, which dissolves blood clots, but only affects people who had mutations on both copies of the gene. Instead, those with one copy of the gene have a longer than average lifespan and 10 percent longer telomeres. Due to these findings, research is underway to investigate if a therapeutic agent that causes PAI- 1 inhibition could potentially slow the effects of aging.

What if I Don't Have Good Genes?

Don't despair if you are not blessed with the perfect genes for longevity. The Danish Twin Study established that only about 20 percent of how long we live is controlled by our genes, whereas the other 80 percent is dictated by our lifestyle.[4] To restate an earlier quote:

Genes load the gun, while the
environment pulls the trigger.

Lessons from the Cuban Embargo

For someone struggling to survive a high stress lifestyle, poverty, lack of food and childhood abuse, even the luckiest genes won't overcome severe and harmful conditions. Yet, even with detrimental genes, you can mitigate their effect and have a positive impact on your health and longevity.

Certain times when populations have suffered harsh conditions offer insights into the impact of the environment on our health. From 1991 to 1995, Cuba was hit particularly hard by an international embargo, creating food shortages, and forcing Cubans to mainly walk and cycle because of the lack of petrol. This led to a population-wide weight loss of about 5.5 kg/12lbs and clear and rapid reductions in mortality from diabetes and coronary heart disease.[5]

In 1995, as the Cuban economy began to recover, obesity resurged and with it diabetes and heart diseases. Researchers say the resurgence was mainly due to an increased consumption of food and drink since physical activity only marginally declined. Energy intake reached pre-crisis levels by 2002 and obesity rates tripled that of 1995 by 2011.

The population-wide increase in weight was immediately followed by a 116 percent increase in diabetes prevalence and 140 percent increase in diabetes incidence. Six years into the weight rebound phase, deaths from diabetes increased by 49 percent.

Calorie Restriction and Longevity

The Cuban experience is a striking example of the positive effect that calorie restriction (but not starvation) has on human health and longevity, and the negative effects of over-consumption of food.

To date, the most effective non-genetic intervention for aging at a cellular level has been **calorie restriction** (CR). This involves eating a well-balanced, and nutrient dense diet that reduces calorie intake by 20 to 40 percent without malnutrition.

Multiple studies of CR in animal and human models have shown a reduction in chronic diseases of aging and an increase in lifespan. This means CR achieves our major goal—increasing the length of time in which we are healthy.

One of the longest human studies was the **CALERIE-2 study**, which followed 220 healthy, young to middle-aged people (21-51 years old) to see how they responded to a

CR diet.[6] The results published in 2016 showed that CR decreased chronic disease risk factors.

For the study, there were two groups: a 25 percent reduction Calorie Restricted diet and a free eating control group. After two years, the CR group lost an average of 7.6kg/16.7lbs, of which 71 percent was fat mass, compared to little or no significant change in the control group.

However, the study participants struggled with full adherence and the researchers concluded that an average CR at 8–10 percent was more achievable over two years.[7]

It's important to note that calorie-restriction regimens **are not starvation diets**. The weight loss achieved with calorie restriction in the CALERIE trial resulted in body weights that were within the normal or overweight range.

The CR group also had significantly improved moods, reduced anxiety, better general health, increased sex drive, as well as improved sleep duration.

A follow-up study two years after the intervention ended found that the participants had sustained most of the weight loss.

The CR group also had reduced risk factors (lower blood pressure and lower cholesterol) for age-related diseases such as diabetes, heart disease, and stroke, with decreases in some inflammatory factors and thyroid hormones.

A *Little Stress is a Good Thing*

It is thought that calorie restriction works because when you starve an organism, it reacts by switching its cells into a highly protected, non-growth mode. It then has a cellular clear-out, hunkering down to recycle resources and rid the cells of any junk. If the nutrient restriction goes on for more than 48 hours, there is evidence that stem cell renewal takes place as well.

If, however, the organism starts to go into starvation mode, then the body hunkers down further. The immune system becomes repressed, the basal metabolism rate is lowered, and it can become nutrient deficient causing fatigue and 'brain-fog". During studies on starvation diets, they found that subjects also became obsessed with food and were continually cold.[8]

Hormesis

The positive effect of calorie restriction is thought to be caused by **hormesis**, which is a biological phenomenon whereby a beneficial effect (improved health, stress tolerance, growth or longevity) results from exposure to low doses of an agent that is otherwise toxic or lethal when given at higher doses, or conditions that invoke a stress response but without causing harm.

When we enter a calorie restricted state, it causes enough of a defense response that our cells restore and replenish themselves without causing harm.

As we saw earlier, our bodies evolved to switch between the two states–fed and fasted–but because today so many of us are stuck in the fed state, we suffer from chronic diseases, while a good portion of the world's population suffer illnesses caused by deprivation.

Living a healthy life span requires keeping our cells robust by staying in a healthy weight range, keeping a balance between fed and fasted states, eating food that is nourishing, regular movement and exercise, reducing inflammation caused by illness, and finding ways to manage chronic stress.

SUMMARY

For a lifelong longevity practice integrate the lifestyle habits of our friends from the Blue Zones

- Make sure exercise is part of your daily life.
- Find your sense of purpose.
- Be mindful and develop strategies to manage stress.
- Follow the 80% Rule. *Eat until you're 80 percent full.*
- Consider a diet that is primarily vegetarian.
- Moderate your alcohol consumption–just one or two glasses per day with family, friends and food.
- Find a faith-based community to engage with or consider getting involved with a service-based group that is dedicated to helping others.
- Focus on family and make them a priority.
- Find friends that are aligned with your goals and support healthy behaviors.

Chapter 19
A Whole Life Approach

Building on the information gained from the Blue Zones study, scientists are unearthing important clues that are going to have a significant impact on our longevity and support our quest to live healthier for longer.

Addressing aging literally begins in the womb, and as we grow our life falls into three distinct phases:

Phase one: Growth and development.
Phase Two: Maintenance
Phase Three: Repair and renewal.

Phase One: Creating a Healthy Foundation

Ideally, phase one should begin with our grandparents, as the healthier parents and grandparents are, the healthier a child will be. Unlike the case of Cuba, where food shortages improved the health of adults, deprivation while in the womb can cause damaging genetic changes that affect a child for life. An increasing body of evidence has found that poor nutrition at the very beginning of life causes large and long- term negative consequences for both mental and physical health. People who are conceived or were in the womb during periods of starvation and famine have long-term changes to their DNA.[1]

The effects of famine appeared to depend on its timing during gestation, and what organs and tissues were undergoing critical periods of development at the time.

Early gestation seems to be the most vulnerable period. People who were conceived during famines are at increased risk of schizophrenia and depression, are more responsive to stress and have a doubled rate of coronary heart disease. Additionally, they perform worse on cognitive tasks, which may be a sign of accelerated aging. People exposed during any period of gestation also have a higher incidence of type 2 diabetes.

The importance of good nutrition in development and early childhood is clear as having healthy growth and development also ensures our cellular health continues as we age.

Phase Two: Maintenance

As we head out of the growth phase, generally in our mid-twenties, we are at our peak fitness and our goal should be a lifestyle that maintains our ongoing health. These are our peak reproductive years when cells are geared towards ensuring we stay as healthy as possible to ensure the best chance for our offspring's survival. This is the time to lay down the good habits and lifestyle to carry us through our prime years and set us up for healthy aging in our later years.

Yet, diseases of aging can also begin here, with some people starting to develop conditions such Alzheimer's disease, cancer, and heart disease in their 30s and 40s.

Everyone will be familiar with the occasional horror story of someone in this age range dying far too early due to a heart attack. It's important to have a regular check up with your doctor to ensure you identify whether you have any risk factors for these conditions. If there are any areas of concern, you can chart a plan to minimize your risk by adapting your lifestyle and potentially undergoing treatment.

Once you have the all-clear then you should proactively focus on the steps you need to take to keep yourself in good working order. As early as your twenties, this begins with exercise and a moderate diet.

Once you hit your 30s, keep up your exercise and moderate diet but consider a strategy of taking supplements that look after the primary Hallmarks of Aging, with the goal of keeping your cellular function and activity in good working order as possible for as long as possible. This means focusing on supporting DNA repair and maintenance, maintaining your telomere length, and supporting healthy levels of DNA methylation to optimize gene regulation and cells function.

Once you hit your 40s, our mitochondria start to noticeably decline, and you should consider supplements to support their function. **NAD-boosting**[2] compounds appear to be the most effective option and are shown to have positive benefits across a range of conditions that start to appear in our 40s.

Taken in conjunction with the DNA support from your 30s, this sets your cells up to maintain healthy DNA as well as giving your cells an energy top-up to ensure repair and maintenance of your cells and cell structures.

Phase Three: Repair and Renewal

Generally, in our mid to late 40s, we start experiencing aches and pains, and changes in our body that we associate with aging.

At this stage it becomes essential to stimulate autophagy, which helps the body clear out proteins and senescent cells, as well as trigger stem cell renewal to refresh those cells that have been removed.

Exercise remains a key mechanism to trigger autophagy. If you are at a healthy weight and are non-diabetic, then consider intermittent fasting or the fasting mimicking diet to boost this process. The fasting mimicking diet provides you with nutrition but tricks your body into thinking it is fasting for 3 to 5 days. Research has shown clear benefits to our health if we fast once every three months, especially for those with autoimmune disorders. Lastly, there are supplements that can inhibit or stimulate key pathways to help you maintain healthy levels of autophagy to clear out faulty proteins and senescent cells.

Read on to learn more about the strategies you can adopt to set yourself up for a long healthy vital life!

CHAPTER 20
A HEALTHY LIFE STRATEGY

Forewarned is forearmed, as they say, and I am going to run you through the information you need to ensure your long health strategy is one that best suits your body and lifestyle.

We start putting aside money for our retirement from the start of our working careers and accelerate that effort as we can over our life. With what we now know, is it is possible to do the same with our health.

Money compounds through investment every day, week, month and year, and our health and longevity does the same. It needn't be difficult, requiring hours in the gym, but with small steps every day that will give you the best chance of a long life.

Know Your DNA Profile

Knowing the risks in your inherited DNA will help you develop the appropriate intervention to offset them. As we saw before, our DNA expression is hugely affected by environment, so knowing what lies in our code helps determine how we can identify negative traits and boost the positive ones.

The first step is to find out your family history, learning what health concerns our parents and grandparents had, whether there is a family history of cancer, cardiovascular disease, Alzheimer's disease and so on.

Knowing your ethnic origins is important as there are genetic conditions that are more common in different ethnic groups, such as sickle cell disease, in people of African, African American, or Mediterranean heritage; and Tay-Sachs disease, among people of Ashkenazi (eastern and central European) Jewish or French-Canadian ancestry.

Gene Testing

For some people, it may not difficult to obtain a family history, so gene testing can help you fill in the gaps. These tests are now widespread and affordable, with testing covering an array of makers for problematic and positive health traits. Many companies offer gene testing for health as much as for tracing family legacy. This can help you identify any family traits that may cause disease, any recessive genes or carrier genes that have been identified as high-risk factors in diseases such as cystic fibrosis development.

A DNA gene test can identify your genetic predisposition for such things as:

- Type 2 diabetes
- Age-related macular degeneration
- Alpha-1 Antitrypsin deficiency (leading to lung and liver disease)
- BRCA1/BRCA2 gene (increased risk of certain cancers)
- Celiac disease
- Familial hypercholesterolemia (Genetic risk for very high cholesterol, which can increase the risk for heart disease)
- Late-onset Alzheimer's disease (APOE gene mutation) Genetic risk for a form of dementia
- Parkinson's Disease. Two variants in the LRRK2 and GBA genes.

Most gene testing companies also offer health wellness reports based on your DNA profile to identify factors such as genetic predisposition to weight loss, muscle composition, deep sleep, lactose intolerance and so on. Shop around to see which one suits you, and once you have taken the initial DNA test, you can request other tests as you want them.

If you decide to go for gene testing, be aware that sometimes they can deliver unpleasant news, so consider having a support person with you if you suspect you may be at risk of a faulty gene and follow up with your doctor if it highlights any areas of concern, such as the BRCA1/ BRCA2 genes.

However, if all goes well, knowing your DNA profile will help you decide which interventions will benefit you the most as far as controlling insulin, weight, your appropriate diet etc.

Please note that having a DNA test is a nice to have, not a need to have. While you will benefit with the knowledge that comes from a test, the reality is that undertaking the activities suggested below will deliver benefits to you regardless of the DNA you have been blessed with.

Your Personal Health Profile

The next step is creating your personal health profile. Do this for yourself, as there is a tendency for people to overstate the positive and understate the negative when filling out health profiles for health insurance and exercise plans. We don't like to admit to others how much we really weigh, that we drink more than two glasses of wine a day or ate an entire block of chocolate on the weekend.

This is the information you need at a minimum:

Age:
Gender:
Current weight–be honest!
Current Body Mass Index: (This can be easily measured using online calculators)
Underweight = <18.5 Normal weight = 18.5–24.9
Overweight = 25–29.9
Obesity = BMI of 30 or greater

Although BMI is not a perfect measure, it is generally agreed to be the most useful and valid for adults (18 years and over). However, there are limitations. For instance, it is less accurate as an indicator of overweight in adults with higher than normal levels of lean body tissue (muscle mass). This is because muscle weighs more than fat and the BMI does factor this in.

It is less accurate as an indicator of being overweight in ethnic groups with smaller body stature (for example, Asian ethnic groups).

Along with BMI, measuring your waist circumference can help you to determine whether you are carrying excess weight around your middle as well as your risk of heart disease and type 2 diabetes.

Waist Circumference

Measuring your waist circumference helps screen for possible health risks that come with being overweight and obesity. If most of your fat is around your waist rather than at your hips, you're at a higher risk for heart disease and Type 2 diabetes. This risk goes up with a waist size that is greater than 35 inches for women or greater than

40 inches for men. To correctly measure your waist, stand and place a tape measure around your middle, just above your hipbones. Measure your waist just after you breathe out.

Drugs And Alcohol

Smoking/Nonsmoking:
Alcohol consumption per week:

Diet

Portions of fruits and vegetables a week:
Portions of meat consumption per week:
How often do you eat? Two to three times daily? Four to six times daily?
Do you snack between meals?
What is the length of time between meals and snacks?

Macronutrients

This may be tricky but try to estimate the percentage of carbohydrate, protein and fat you consume each day. Break it down into categories such as carbohydrates like bread, rice, pasta etc., plant-based and meat-based protein, and the amount of fruit and vegetables, you eat in a day. If you are not sure which category a food in your diet sits then a quick search on the internet will tell you.

How many sugary drinks do you consume, such as soda, fruit juice, sweet iced tea, milk shakes?

Do you have any food allergies or intolerances?

Exercise

How often do you exercise per week? What types of exercise do you do?

Stress Management

How would you describe your ability to manage stress?
What do you do for stress management?
Do you set aside time for self-care?

Social Networks

How supportive are your social networks?
Do you have access to emotional support if you need it?
Do you have someone you can call if you need help and support?

Immune System Status

Have you been vaccinated for common infectious diseases?
Do you get a regular influenza vaccination?
Have you had chicken pox, shingles or HPV vaccine?
Do you get sufficient sleep?

This list is simply to prompt you to start thinking about your own health status. You don't have to share it with anyone so be brutally honest, because in the next section I am going to help you construct a life plan that suits your life stage, lifestyle and resources.

Resources

People often fail to consider the resources available to them when developing health plans. A busy parent with young children in an apartment, or a student working a part-time job while studying may not have the time or budget to go the gym or for a walk in the park three times a week. No matter people's best intentions, most of us fail to stick to health and exercise plans because we overestimate our resources.

I want you to consider the resources and time you have available to you on a weekly basis that will let you exercise and improve your diet.

If you are stuck inside because it is the middle of winter, you can use YouTube exercise videos, stationary bikes, even dancing for exercise. What works for you in your time frame and budget? (By the way, dancing is a quick and easy way to get started exercising if the thought of burpees and push-ups makes your blood run cold).

Support

What support do you need to get started? This is different from resources. For example, if you want to stop smoking, what support do you need to stop? If you want to eat healthier food, but come home exhausted and order take out, how could you make it easier to ensure healthier food is easily available? Is it just habit? How can you break those habits?

Set Some Goals

What is your Healthy Aging goal? Do you want to live to be a hundred, or are you happy to be a healthy 75-year-old?

Do you have specific concerns about disorders of aging like arthritis, heart disease and Alzheimer's disease that you want to stave off?

Give its some thought and make it a priority. The small steps you take today will pay off. People often talk about their bad habits but instead write down all the good habits you have and build from there.

The Effect of Compounding

It's never too early or too late to start healthy living, and remember the key is small incremental changes every day that add up over time like compounding interest. Reducing the amount of fast food you eat, going for a walk once or twice a week, and cutting down on the sugar in your diet will start to add up and as you see results, it will encourage you to build on them.

CHAPTER 21
BUILD YOUR HEALTHY AGING STRATEGY

Now that you have developed your personal life profile, work your way through the table below to identify the areas you want to bolster. For each Hallmark there is a lifestyle, environmental, nutritional and supplement intervention to prevent, manage or repair it. Not all of them may be applicable to you, so if you are overweight, and at risk of developing Type 2 diabetes, you will want to look at interventions that help control blood sugar and bring your weight down. If you are a student in your 20s who exercises regularly, maintaining your DNA integrity and telomere length as you age will be more relevant.

Hallmark	Intervention
Genomic instability	Exercise, non-smoking, moderate diet, moderate to no alcohol consumption
Telomere attrition	Reduce stress (mindfulness and mediation can slow telomere shortening)
Epigenetic alterations	Include foods rich in folate (leafy greens) in your diet
Mitochondrial dysfunction	Reduce avoid certain medicines that affect mitochondrial function, exercise regularly
Stem cell fatigue	Eat a wide range of foods that contain different flavonoids (eat the rainbow of organic fruit and vegetables)
Intercellular communication	Exercise, non-smoking, moderate diet, moderate alcohol consumption
Cellular senescence	Exercise and the range of different fasting methods that support the removal of senescent cells from the body
Loss of proteostasis	Exercise and the range of different fasting methods that support the removal of senescent cells from the body
Deregulated nutrient sensing	Exercise and the range of different fasting methods that support the removal of senescent cells from the body

Supplements	
Supplements that support DNA repair mechanisms	NR, NMN, 2-Hoba, Resveratrol, Pterostilbene, rutin + Vitamin C, Vitamin D, selenium and zinc
Supplements that support telomere length and reduced oxidative stress in the cells	Astragaloside A, astaxanthin, resveratrol, pterostilbene
Supplements that deliver methyl groups to your cells or support key enzymes involved in methylation	5methytetrahydrofolate, SAMe, Curcumin + Vit C
Supplement with NAD boosting compounds and those that support optimal mitochondrial function	NR, NMN, apigenin, rutin, quercetin, astaxanthin, B Vitamins, Carnosine, Alpha Lipoic Acid
Supplement with concentrated flavanoid compounds and supplements that support mitochondrial function	NR, NMN, apigenin, rutin, quercetin, astaxanthin, B Vitamins, carnosine, Alpha Lipoic Acid
Supplement with NAD boosting compounds	Olueropein, astragaloside A, withaferin A, NMN, apigenin
Supplement with compounds known to moderately inhibit mTor and activate AMPK to mimic calorie restriction and trigger autophagy	Berberine, withaferin A, ECGC, fisetin
Supplement with compounds known to moderately inhibit mTor and activate AMPK to mimic calorie restriction and trigger autophagy	Oleuropein, berberine, withaferin A, fisetin, ECGC
Supplement with compounds known to moderately inhibit mTor and activate AMPK to mimic calorie restriction and trigger autophagy	Berberine, withaferin A, ECGC, fisetin

Hallmark	Priority	Age 20	30-39	40-49	50+
Genomic instability		x	x	x	x
Telomere attrition		x	x	x	x
Epigenetic alterations		x	x	x	x
Mitochondrial dysfunction				x	x
Stem cell fatigue				x	x
Intercellular communication				x	x
Cellular senescence					x
Loss of proteostasis					x
Deregulated nutrient sensing					x

Your Thirties

Protect Your DNA

Reduce your exposure to carcinogens that cause DNA damage leading to replication errors and mutations. The earlier we start this in life the better.

DNA is often damaged because of spontaneous errors during cell division, but there are numerous substances in our environment that can directly damage our DNA. Anything considered carcinogenic (that is, cancer-causing) is also mutagenic (causes mutations) and associated with various forms of DNA damage.

These agents either directly cause DNA damage, such as double strand breaks, or link with other chemicals in our bodies that cause the damage.

Ionizing Radiation (X-rays)

Ionizing radiation[1] directly damages DNA, particularly causing double strand breaks. High exposure to radiation causes rapid onset of radiation sickness and death, as seen after nuclear accidents such as the Chernobyl reactor failure in the Ukraine. People who received high doses of radiation died within three months of the accident, while those exposed to lower doses developed cancer over the next few years.

Fortunately, nuclear accidents are rare, and the highest exposure risk most people have is through medical radiation treatment. Radiotherapy and x-rays are well-studied and safe forms of treatment, but it is important

---

1 Ionizing radiation differs from electromagnetic radiation in that it can break chemical bonds.

to understand the risks so always ask health providers for guidelines to ensure your exposure remains at safe levels.

Ultraviolent Radiation (Sun Damage)

It's easy to see the effect of UV radiation on our bodies; simply compare the skin on your wrist to the top of your arm. Skin cancer rates are associated with sunlight exposure and damage from sunburn. Melanoma of the skin is the nineteenth most common cancer and rates in Australasia are the highest in the world. This is thought to be due to having a large proportion of fair-skinned people living in countries with high levels of sunshine. Fortunately, attitudes have changed since the 1960s and 70s when having a tan was considered fashionable. Preventing sun damage from an early age is vital, so to reduce your risk, use a sunscreen with an SPF of 15 or higher, avoid the sun between 10am and 4pm, and cover up with a t-shirt and broad-brimmed hat while in the sun.

Vitamin D

However, not all sun exposure is bad as our bodies make Vitamin D when our skin is exposed to sunshine, so try for 10-20 minutes a day when the sun is less harsh, before 10am and after 4 pm, although this can depend on the season and latitude. If this is not possible, consider Vitamin D supplementation.

Air Pollution–Polycyclic Aromatic Hydrocarbons (PAHs)

Burning organic matter causes generation of PAHs. They are found in smoke from fires, car exhausts, tobacco smoke, and industrial pollution. PAHs are the most abundant indirect- acting carcinogens to which humans are exposed to daily. Exposure has been associated with the development of breast, skin and lung cancer. Air pollution causes 9 percent of deaths globally and is one of the leading risk factors for disease burden.

How to reduce exposure to PAHs? It's not easy in big cities but try to live away from main roads. If that's not feasible, then live in a house that is as far as possible from the road. If you enjoy walking and running do these activities during non-peak traffic hours or off-road, far away from vehicle exhaust.

Heterocyclic Aromatic Amines (HAAs)

HAAs are considered some of the strongest known mutagens and arise during the cooking of meats, fish, and poultry. Several HAAs are also found in tobacco smoke and diesel exhaust. They typically form at high temperatures and studies have found that frequent consumption of well-done cooked meats containing HAAs can elevate the risks for colon, prostate, and mammary cancers. Reducing our intake of roasted meat and changing cooking methods can limit our exposure to HAAs. (Also see Advanced Glycation End Products and how to cook to limit your exposure).

Nitrosamines

Nitrosamines are common in water and foods, including cured and grilled meats, dairy products and vegetables. Everyone is exposed to some level of nitrosamines, and they are also found in some medications. As foods and drugs are processed in the body, nitrosamines can also be formed. Nitrosamine impurities may increase the risk of cancer if people are exposed to them above acceptable levels or over long periods of time.

Fortunately, as the risks have become known, nitrite-free products are now available so look for them when shopping for your favorite deli meats.

Stop Smoking

Smoking tobacco cigarettes directly damages our DNA, suppresses the immune system and causes inflammation–and it is incredibly aging.

When tobacco smoke enters our lungs, it exposes the delicate lung tissue to at least 60 powerful chemical carcinogens with the potential to cause DNA damage to larynx, bronchi, and lung epithelial cells.

The tar and nicotine contained in cigarettes also have immunosuppressive effects on the innate immune response and tobacco products containing high concentrations of tar and nicotine cause the greatest immunologic changes.

Chronic inflammation is considered a major consequence of smoking that causes increased cell proliferation in the exposed lung tissue, which may ultimately result in cancer cells.

CHAPTER 22
BOOSTING DNA

Now it's time to look at what science is telling us about supporting our health and function of our DNA.

It is a recurring theme in this book, but exercise is a key strategy to help support your DNA function and support the DNA repair mechanisms that we all have in our cells. It really is the best thing you can do today to help your health journey. A few minutes a day is all that is needed if exercise is not part of your life right now but work towards 30 minutes a day.

A good diet and finding ways to manage stress are also key.

We also now have tools at our disposal that support healthy DNA function.

BOOST DNA REPAIR SYSTEMS

NAD

As we saw in Hallmark One, the SIRTUIN genes in our cells act as our DNA repair crew. This group of genes is NAD (nicotinamide adenine dinucleotide) dependent, meaning they need NAD to function.

In the mitochondria, NAD helps convert glucose to energy, while in our cells raised levels of NAD+ directs enzymes, including the SIRTUINs, to make adjustments to ensure cell survival through energy production and utilization, boosting cellular repair, and coordinating circadian rhythms.

When we are young, NAD+ is plentiful as our body makes and recycles it, but as we age it declines so that by the time we reach our sixties, NAD+ levels in our bodies have halved.

Boosting NAD+

Our body produces NAD+ from vitamin B3, niacin and the amino acid tryptophan, while nicotinic acid, nicotinamide, and tryptophan are NAD+ precursors. Nicotinic acid and nicotinamide are both forms of niacin (Vitamin B3). However, too much niacin can cause uncomfortable flushing, and more niacin doesn't make for higher NAD+ levels. Nicotinamide, a form of vitamin B3 that doesn't cause flushing, helps support NAD+ metabolism, but high doses don't directly boost NAD+ levels. The same applies to tryptophan. You need enough in your diet to support NAD+, but taking more doesn't raise levels.

However, three main NAD+ boosters are the subject of intense research:

- **NR–Nicotinamide riboside chloride**
- **NMN–Nicotinamide mononucleotide**
- **NADH–Nicotinamide adenine dinucleotide hydride**

They are all precursors of NAD+ that work to raise its levels and are easily to obtain as supplements.

Sirtuin Activating Compounds (STACs)

Resveratrol and Pterostilbene

Resveratrol and pterostilbene (found in blueberries) have also been found to slow aging, and work synergistically with NR or NMN, to boost NAD+ levels.

Resveratrol is a polyphenol found mainly in red grapes, red wine, red grape juice, peanuts and some berries. It is produced by plants in response to mechanical injury, UV radiation and pathogens, such as bacteria and fungi. Resveratrol possesses a wide range of biological properties, among them antioxidant, cardioprotective, neuroprotective, anti-inflammatory and anticancer activities, which attracted a lot of attention when its potential was first identified.

Unluckily, a major issue for its use as a supplement is its poor solubility and bioavailability, so other forms have been investigated.

Pterostilbene is a natural resveratrol analogue, first isolated from *Pterocarpus santalinus* (red sandalwood). The Pterocarpus marsupium active constituent is mainly found in blueberries, grapes, and several plant woods, and has better bioavailability than resveratrol.

The Enzyme CD38 and NAD

There is also another way to boost your NAD and it's something that not many people are aware of. It turns out that as we get older and accumulate extra weight, we also accumulate inflammatory cells that have raised levels of an enzyme called CD38, a **NADase**, which is a protein that consumes NAD[1].

When scientists removed CD38 in mice, they discovered the mice had higher levels of NAD+ and increased SIRT1 activity.

This may happen because CD38 is also involved in the immune response. It seems when cells become senescent, they also express higher levels of CD38, which uses up NAD precursors and in turn lowers NAD+. As more cells become senescent, this pushes up CD38 levels, which in turn drives down NAD+, reducing the availability for cellular metabolism and DNA repair activity of the SIRTUINs.

As always, the Hallmarks are heavily intertwined. Reducing the number of senescent cells lowers inflammation, which in turn prevents CD38 levels rising and using up NAD+. This lets the SIRTUINs do their repair work and reduces the stress on our tissues.

Unfortunately, if you are overweight and taking NAD boosting supplements you are probably not getting the full benefit. But there is a way to resolve this.

The Power of Flavonoids

Research is underway to discover safe ways to inhibit CD38, but a class of natural compounds have been found to not only modify CD38 but also to have wide range of positive effect on our cells and tissues., In fact, fruits and vegetables contain substantial quantities of molecules that have multiple health benefits, which is why they should always form part of our diet. So, how do we reduce CD38 levels? The secret is in your salad!

Flavonoids are a diverse group of phytonutrients (plant chemicals) found in fruits, vegetables, grains, bark, roots, stems, flowers, tea and wine. More than 4000 varieties of flavonoids have been identified.

There are six major subclasses of flavonoids, namely anthocyanidins, flavan-3-ols, flavanols, flavanones, flavones, and isoflavones. **Flavanols** are the most widespread in the human diet, and eating fruits and vegetables are the main source of flavonoids, along with drinking teas and wine.

Flavonoids give plants their color as well as performing important functions such as attracting pollinating insects;

combating environmental stresses, such as microbial infection; and regulating cell growth.

Although it was initially thought that the biological effects of flavonoids were related to their antioxidant activity, but further studies suggests that many of the effects of flavonoids, including anti-inflammatory, antidiabetic, anticancer, and neuro-protective activities, are related to their ability to modulate cell-signaling pathways.[2] And it turns out that flavonoids are master CD38 inhibitors.

CD38 *Inhibitors*

Several naturally occurring compounds are also reported to inhibit the activity of CD38 including flavonoid compounds[3]:

Apigenin is a common dietary flavonoid that is abundant in many fruits and vegetables, is the most effective at inhibiting CD38. It has multiple physiological functions, such as strong anti-inflammatory, antioxidant, antibacterial and antiviral activities and blood pressure reduction. It is found in parsley, grapes, apples, grapefruit, oranges, chamomile and red wine.

Quercetin is found in many fruits, vegetables. Leaves, seeds, and grains; capers, buckwheat, red onions and kale are common foods containing appreciable amounts of quercetin.

Luteolin is found in vegetables and fruits such as celery, parsley, broccoli, onion leaves, carrots, green peppers, cabbages, apple skins, and pumpkin are luteolin rich.

Callistephin is an anthocyanin, which is a type of flavonoid that may appear red, purple, blue or black. Food plants rich in anthocyanins include pomegranates, blueberries, raspberries, black rice, and black soybeans.

Kuromanin is another anthocyanin found in mulberry leaves, blackcurrants, red raspberries, lychees, and Peruvian purple corn.

What this shows is the unmistakable benefits of eating a varied diet, rich in fruits and vegetable, so make sure to eat all the colors!

A New Tool for DNA protection

2-Hoba

There is one compound that I have come across that is notable for its ability to protect DNA and convey significant benefits to our cells. It is a compound isolated from Himalayan Tartary Buckwheat, which has been part of the diet of people living in the Himalayas for eons and has more recently become widely accessible. This is a compound has novel benefit for our health and acts to protect biological molecules from oxidative stress in a way that has not been available before.

Known as 2-Hoba, it gives all the health benefits of antioxidants without the risks. As we outlined earlier, antioxidants are molecules that neutralize reactive oxygen species (or free radicals). What we have learnt over the past decade is that not all free radicals are bad and that our cells actually use them for many beneficial purposes, including intracellular signaling, and immune response.

It turns out that we can harm to our cells if we take too many antioxidants as it reduces our cells' ability to use free radicals beneficially as antioxidants can remove the bad free radicals, but also the good ones as well.

What makes 2-Hoba unique is that it gives us all the benefits of protecting our critical cellular machinery, membranes and DNA without interfering with the healthy and beneficial effects of free radicals.

Whilst the discoverers of 2-Hoba are only a decade into their research, the compound is already showing remarkable health benefits and it is an exciting breakthrough in our tool kit for compounds that protect our DNA from damage and lowering the burden on our DNA repair systems.

Chapter 23
Maintaining Telomere Length

Looking after our DNA and protecting our telomeres march hand and hand. Although our telomeres may have a pre-ordained length, we can slow and prevent accelerated attrition with our lifestyle choices.[1]

To recap, telomeres shorten with each cell division and determine how fast our cells age and when they die, according to how fast they wear down.

Telomeres are Blackburn's area of expertise, and her research team found that external factors such as stress shorten our telomeres faster by studying the telomeres of care givers.

Their research has shown that caring for chronically sick and disabled people can shorten the life expectancy of the care giver by six years or more. After analyzing the telomeres of a group of mothers with chronically ill children, Blackburn discovered the caregivers who perceived themselves as being under the most stress also had the shortest telomeres.

This indicated to them that telomere length can be influenced by the external environment, and indeed subsequent research has found that lifestyle can influence telomere length within three weeks.

Blackburn concluded that how we manage and respond to stress has a profound effect on our telomere length and the speed at which we age. A small amount of stress won't damage our telomeres, but chronic stress that continues for a substantial amount of time will.

However, Blackburn says it is not the stress itself that causes the damage, but the stress response. Her studies found that it was one type of stress response that affected telomeres the most—the threat response.

The Threat Response

You are home by yourself, it's late at night and very dark outside. Suddenly a door creaks, something bangs against the wall and before you know it your heart is pounding and opening the door seems the most terrifying act in the world. You contemplate going to check, but instead huddle down under your blankets, jumping at every bang and squeak for hours. In the morning, you go outside and discover a chair fell over in the wind—no big deal. So why were you so afraid? Let's break that scenario down.

We are all familiar with this scenario because it is an ancient response hard-wired into our nervous systems and more commonly described as the fight/flight/freeze response.

When our brain perceives a stimulus as a threat, it triggers a cascade of reactions to prepare us to either run, stand and fight or freeze. Initiated by a signal from the amygdala in our brain, the hormones adrenaline and cortisol are released, increasing our blood pressure, blood sugar and suppressing the immune system to give us an energy boost. Our heart beats faster, our digestion stops, and we have increased blood flow and muscle tension.

The problem with the threat response is that it is only meant to be short term to deal with an immediate threat. Unfortunately for modern humans, the stress of our daily lives can lead to continual activation of the threat response, causing chronic stress. It is the ongoing high levels of adrenaline and cortisol, and the activation of the sympathetic nervous system that wears us and our telomeres down.

Stress is part of life, and in small doses it is good for us so learning how to manage and respond to stress has a profound impact on our wellbeing. Fortunately, the effect of chronic stress on our health is now well recognized and there are numerous techniques and guides we can use to help us to manage and respond to it better, including:

- Social support
- Regular exercise
- Meditation/prayer/mindfulness
- Yoga
- Hobbies
- Active relaxation
- Being in nature
- Rest

The first step is acknowledging that stress is something we all face and need to manage and seek out the techniques that work best with your time and resources.

Telomere Support Supplements

In addition to the above, consider taking supplements that boost NAD, SIRTUIN activators such as resveratrol or pterostilbene, and telomerase activators like *astragalus*, a Chinese herb whose active component Astragaloside has been shown to support telomere length and is well known for its health properties.[2]

IN SUMMARY

In your thirties a key priority is to support and maintain your DNA

- Exercise, diet and minimizing stress.
- Add in a SIRTUIN activator like resveratrol or pterostilbene
- Add in a NAD boosting supplement (remember SIRTUINs need NAD to function optimally)
- If you are overweight, then add in apigenin to make sure you are getting optimal levels of NAD
- Take astragalus to support telomere length and methyl donors to help support regulate epigenetic modulation of your genes.
- Take 2Hoba for extra protection for your DNA (and all your cellular machinery)

Chapter 24
Your Forties

Supporting Mitochondrial Function

Virtually all our energy needs are produced by the mitochondria contained in our cells. They are so small, a billion could fit on a grain of sand and our cells can contain hundreds of mitochondria each, meaning we have quadrillions of mitochondria producing the adenosine triphosphate (ATP) needed to power our cells.

And produce they do. There is no off switch for mitochondria, as ATP has to be continually produced because it can't be stored. A healthy person at rest produces their body weight in ATP every day, or when exercising, up 0.5 to 1.0 kg/2.2lbs per minute.

As discussed in Hallmark Six, the main source of oxidative stress in our cells is free radical species of oxygen and high-energy electrons leaking from the mitochondria.

Mitochondrial reactive oxygen leakage is a strong predictor across species for longevity—the better a species is at protecting its mitochondria, the longer it lives.[1] Unfortunately, this leakage increases as we age, and it's a key reason why we start losing energy in our forties and the down-stream effects of less energy on our cells have a material impact on our cell health.

---

1 This is why some birds like parrots have very long lives for their size as they have great free radical management systems.

There are many strategies for improving your mitochondrial health and function and, you guessed it, the best place to start is with exercise. When you exercise your body signals that it needs more energy triggering certain pathways designed to increase the numbers of mitochondria in your cells.

Interestingly, cold therapy also useful as it increases the numbers and function of mitochondria in your fat turning white fat cells into metabolically active brown fat cells. Cold therapy can be done simply at home by having a couple of cold showers per week or daily if you can. Google the Wim Hof Method and visit Wim's website to learn more about the benefits associated with being cold. It's a little hard to start but once you get going it's very addictive!

However, regardless of the benefits of exercise and of cold therapy it is well-documented that mitochondrial function becomes compromised from our forties and worsens gradually over the rest of our life. To help combat this decline, you can take supplements that support mitochondrial function. One of the most effective natural supplements is a unique molecule called astaxanthin.

Astaxanthin

Astaxanthin is a very interesting antioxidant with unique properties that is found in algae. Red in color, it is what gives salmon its lovely color as it is a key part of their diet. Algae need extremely strong antioxidant protection because they are exposed to continuous and extremely high levels of UV as they float on or near the surface of the ocean.

Astaxanthin's structure is unique by having both lipophilic (fat loving) and hydrophilic (water loving) properties. These properties cause it to be attracted to and embed itself into our cellular membranes. And, it turns out that its length is very similar to that of our membranes making astaxanthin the perfect antioxidant to protect the protective membranes that surround our mitochondria.

This is specifically relevant to our mitochondria because they produce almost all of the free radicals in our cells as a byproduct of the energy generating process. This places the biological membranes in our mitochondria right at the source of the free radical generation, and under significant stress. When we are young our mitochondrial membranes have plenty of antioxidants naturally embedded in them but as we age this declines, and the net effect is compromised membranes and compromised mitochondrial function. Research has shown that astaxanthin suppresses oxidative stress-induced mitochondrial dysfunction. Interestingly, it has been found to upregulates the activity of respiratory chain complexes and ATP synthase as well as the level of their main subunits, indicating that astaxanthin not only supports outer mitochondrial membranes but also the important inner mitochondrial membrane as well.

It turns out that astaxanthin is the perfect natural mitochondrial-supporting antioxidant and research is now showing that it has the potential to support all of the conditions associated with the increasing mitochondrial dysfunction associated with aging.

Nicotinamide Mononucelotide (NMN) and Nicotinamide Riboside (NR)

When we last talked about the NAD boosting supplements, NMN and NR, it was because they supported the activity and function of the DNA repairing SIRTUINs 1, 6 and 7. Mitochondria have SIRTUINs as well—3,4 and 5 that are integral to the function of our mitochondria. And because Sirtuins are dependent on NAD then it makes sense that boosting levels of NAD will also support mitochondrial function.

Pterostilbene

Along with boosting your NAD levels, adding in pterostilbene or resveratrol is an equally good strategy to support the function of the SIRTUINs resident in your mitochondria.

IN SUMMARY;

Boosting Mitochondrial Health

- The usual suspects–you know them by now, exercise, diet and stress reduction.
- Take astaxanthin to support mitochondrial function and lower oxidative stress in your cells.
- Take NAD boosting compounds NMN or NR and don't forget, if you are little overweight, to take apigenin to help combat the negative effects of CD38 on your cellular NAD levels.
- Take the SIRTUIN activating compounds resveratrol or pterostilbene.

Chapter 25

Replenishing Stem Cells

By now you can see why healthy cell renewal is key to successful aging and maintaining a healthy stem cell supply is fundamental to this. Studies suggest that a gradual reduction in the number of stem cells in your body acts as a biological clock for aging.

As a refresher, your stem cells are like a repository or bank of cells that are ready to replace cells that have been removed from the body when they are past their best before date. Stem cells are unique compared to your regular cells because they have an ability to turn into other cells as the body needs them.

An example is your bone marrow which holds stem cells that are precursors for the different types of blood cells. Your spinal cord holds neural stem cells ready to be used in your brain when they are needed. You have skin stem cells that can turn in to different skin cells hiding out around your hair follicles and in the base layer of your skin.

Strategies to help our stem cell populations from becoming exhausted include the usual suspects (there is a theme here!) of exercise, reducing oxidative stress and inflammation, maintaining a healthy diet, avoiding certain toxins like smoking and alcohol and keeping stress at manageable levels.

Certain supplements can also help: NR, NMN, apigenin, rutin, quercetin, pterostilbene, astaxanthin, B Vitamins, carnosine, alpha lipoic acid and vitamin D have all be found to help support stem cell function and maintain healthy stem cell populations.

Stem Cell Support

Fasting

Recently fasting was found to support stem cell health. When you fast there are many benefits as we have discussed earlier in the book. But work done by Valter Longo has shown that fasting beyond 72 hours can boost stem cell renewal.[1] Prolonged fasting forces the body to use its stores of glucose, fat and ketones for energy, and also breaks down a significant portion of our cells in a process called autophagy that removes senescent cells then triggers stem cell-based regeneration of new cells once eating starts. In particular, prolonged fasting reduces the enzyme PKA, which is linked to the regulation of stem cell self-renewal and pluripotency—that is, the potential for one cell to develop into many different cell types.

In Summary

To Boost Stem Cell Health:

The usual suspects–exercise, healthy diet and reducing stress.

Take steps to reduce oxidative stress and inflammation including eating a healthy diet, reduce or stop alcohol intake, don't smoke

Consider fasting for 72 hours three to four times per year.

Take key supplements like apigenin, curcumin, vitamin D and NMN.

Chapter 26
Your Fifties

Protein Repair and Maintenance

Autophagy and Cell Repair

In Hallmark Four-Loss of Proteostasis, we saw that autophagy is the quality control process of our cells that removes damaged components. It is one of the body's major repair mechanisms and invoking it through various mechanisms can help us repair and rejuvenate our cells and tissues.

The word autophagy simply means self-eating, and it is the mechanism our body uses to recycle and renew damaged cell components.

Its origins are an ancient survival mechanism that allows organisms to prevent starvation by recycling cell components. In essence, it is a cellular recycling process. When our cells detect low nutrient levels, it triggers signals for the autophagy process to collect up cellular debris and toxic materials for recycling and disposal.

This process is ongoing in our bodies and is much like a cleaning crew in a factory, wandering around tidying up the scraps and broken items left lying around.

Because of its role in clearing away misfolded proteins, senescent cells, damaged mitochondria and toxic cellular debris, it is hoped that autophagy can be harnessed by new therapies to reduce inflammaging, and support longevity.

Autophagy is also activated by DNA damage as part of the DNA Damage Response (DDR) mechanism. The DDR is a network of intracellular pathways that utilize proteins involved in sensing, signaling, and repair of DNA damage. If the cell can't be repaired, it triggers cell death or senescence, and in some cases, autophagy to recycle damaged cells and also trigger mitophagy–the removal and recycling of damaged mitochondria.

Supporting its role in DNA repair are multiple studies that have found reduced autophagy activity can contribute to diseases caused by DNA damage, including cancer and aging. Recognition of the important role autophagy plays in our health and aging has made it the subject of intense research, as it is involved in multiple biological processes including development, cellular renewal, and the immune system. If we can boost autophagy at the right times, then we can reduce the risk factors for aging and chronic diseases.

The Role of mTOR in Autophagy

A key player in the activation of autophagy is mTOR, the nutrient sensing pathway discussed in Hallmark Six. This master controller senses nutrient levels in our cells, especially amino acids, and when they drop too low, one of its responses is to maintain nutrient levels by inducing autophagy. It is the master switch that moves our metabolism between the fed and fasted states. When nutrient levels are high, mTOR activates a growth response, when they are low, we go into maintenance mode.

For healthy aging, we need to move between both states, mainly growth and development when we are younger and then repair and restoration as we age. Inhibiting or activating mTOR is how we can do this, and one of the main ways to do this is through **calorie restriction (CR),** which simply mimics the alternating fed or fasted states our ancestors experienced. Unfortunately, in the modern world we are mostly overfed, jamming mTOR permanently in growth mode, which fuels diseases of aging.

Calorie Restriction and Longevity

As well the mTOR response, Calorie Restriction (CR) also enhances the response of other of other pathways including the IGF-1 pathway, improving insulin sensitivity.

CR exerts an anti-inflammatory effect by inhibiting **nuclear factor-kB,** (NF-kB) a protein complex that controls the transcription of DNA, cytokine production and cell survival.

CR also decreases the production of free radicals and increases mitochondrial biogenesis through different pathways (AMPK, SIRTUINs, and eNOS) leading to improved mitochondrial activity.

The CR-induced activation of FoxO genes assists autophagy and mitophagy and the increased expression of antioxidants.

CR also activates Nuclear factor erythroid 2-related factor 2 (Nrf2) that increases the expression of mitochondrial and cell antioxidant enzymes.

Overall, a reduced calorie intake improves the efficiency of our metabolism and protects our cells against damage. It is thought that this comes from an ancient response aiming to avoid useless expenditure of energy and recycle cell components to ensure survival.[2]

It is evident that CR has a global positive effect on our health, unfortunately it is also a regime that many people find almost difficult to maintain.

Humans love to eat, and for most of us food is part of life. Even within the controlled environment of research studies, the participants have struggled to maintain a long-term calorie-restricted diet. Thankfully, there are other ways to achieve the same effect without having to endure the misery of denial.

Dietary Restriction

A less onerous version is dietary restriction (DR). Numerous studies have found that a high level of protein consumption, especially animal protein, was a risk factor for many chronic diseases. People aged 50 to 65 who had a protein intake more than 20 percent of their total calories had a 75 percent higher risk of death and four-fold higher death rate from cancer and diabetes.

Using protein restriction and dietary restriction of specific amino acids, particularly branched chain amino acids and methionine is an alternate to CR as it mimics some of its beneficial effects.[3]

This applies to particularly to the amino acids methionine, and the branch-chained amino acids (BCAA) arginine, leucine, isoleucine and valine, mainly found in meat, chicken, fish and eggs. These activate mTOR and reducing our intake of them has been shown to improve our health.

An easy way to do this is to increase the number of meat-free meals you have. Even one meat free meal a week is beneficial but aim for three to four. A side benefit of not eating meat is that meat has a much bigger impact on the environment versus a plant-based diet so not only will you gain health benefits, you will lower your environmental impact—a win for you and a win for the planet!

However, this doesn't apply to people over 65, because as we get older our protein needs rise again, and it seems beneficial for people to increase their protein intake to preserve muscle mass. In fact, a higher protein diet coupled with exercise has been found to improve muscle mass in the elderly.

Fasting

An alternate to calorie restriction is fasting, which is growing in popularity as a more manageable way to gain the benefits of calorie restriction without the misery of long-term reduced food intake. The reality is that most people are simply not used to being hungry yet can manage short-term breaks in eating.

Similar to calorie restriction, fasting activates ancient responses in our cells because starvation and nutrient shortages have been part of the life of all organisms for billions of years.

Fasting generally involves drinking only water for a certain period. Prolonged fasting is anything longer than 24 hours, intermittent fasting is generally 16 to 24 hours, or alternate day fasting when you eat one day and not the next.

Fasting in different patterns has been part of human culture for centuries and is observed by most major religions, either for a period, such as Lent or Ramadan, or on particular days.

Fasting induces a number of metabolic responses according to the length of time since the last meal. A person is considered in a fasted state 8–12 hours after last meal and the metabolic changes of the fasting state begin typically 3–5 hours after eating.

What happens to our body when we fast?

12 Hours: We have used up glucose stores and moved into ketosis
24 Hours: Autophagy has begun
48 hours: Growth Hormone levels have increased
53 hours: Insulin sensitivity has improved
72 hours: Breakdown of old immune cells and generation of new stem cells.

The Fasting Mimicking Diet

The fasting mimicking diet (FMD) was developed by Dr Valter Longo as a way to trick the body into thinking it is fasting so that you get all the benefits of a fast without going through quite as much pain as a full fast. Dr Longo discovered that if you consume less than 600 calories a day for a week you get all the benefits of a full fast along with getting to eat a restricted diet to ease the challenge of 5 days off food. I recommend Dr Longo's book, the Longevity Diet, especially for those who are dealing with the challenge of cancer as it seems the combination of his diet with chemotherapy may improve outcomes over the long term.

The Optimal Diet

In between periods of fasting, a diet rich in vegetables, fish, nuts and wholegrains provides us with the protein, carbohydrate and fat, as well as the essential nutrients we need to for good health and is largely the basis of the Mediterranean diet most often cited as the best way to eat.

As with any action you take to improve your longevity and health span, it's important that you undertake CR, DR or fasting under the direction of an expert. Talk with your doctor, pharmacist or nutritionist so that you ensure that you continue to take healthy levels of macro and micronutrients and that you are not overdoing it as that can have equally negative effects on your health.

Fasting Mimicking Supplements

For those who don't like calorie restriction, fasting or diets, some medicines and supplements mimic the effect of Calorie Restriction by inhibiting mTOR. Chief among them is rapamycin, which I discussed in chapter nine. However, this is a powerful drug and not something you should take without medical supervision.

Rapamycin Mimetics

Fortunately, several naturally occurring compounds mimic the action of rapamycin without the potential of adverse side effects.

***Withaferin* A**

Withania somnifera (Ashwagandha) appears to be one of the most effective mTOR inhibitors and this may be how this adaptogenic herb, used for millennia by Ayurvedic medicine practitioners exerts its beneficial health effects

***Epigallocatechin gallate* (EGCG)**

Epigallocatechin-3-gallate (EGCG), is a component extracted from green tea. It is a catechin, which is a type of flavonol found in plants and (such as apples, blueberries, gooseberries, grape seeds, kiwi, strawberries), green tea, red wine, beer, cacao liquor, chocolate, and cocoa.

Metformin

Like rapamycin, the diabetes medication metformin is also an mTOR inhibitor, although indirectly so and via multiple mechanisms. Although metformin inhibits mTOR, it may also reduce free radical leakage in the mitochondria. This action leads, among other things, to beneficial changes in cellular energy status and activation of AMPK. Again, metformin is a prescription medication, but mimetics for metformin include **glucosamine**, a compound used in the treatment of osteoarthritis and **berberine** a compound that is often used by functional medicine doctors as a natural alternative to metformin without the risks and side effects associated with metformin.[4]

Reducing Cellular Senescence

Senescence, as we discussed earlier is the process where cells reach their end of replicative life. Senescent cells are normally removed by our immune system but for whatever reason, as we age our immune system fails to recognize and remove these cells. They accumulate in our body secreting increasing levels of inflammatory mediators and other nasty molecules into neighboring cells and tissues and generally having a negative effect on our health.

Senolytics

Senolytics are a relatively new area of research and describe any compound (drugs, plant extracts, or peptides) or cell-clearing therapies that help to eliminate senescent cells from the body. These include the flavins (derived from black tea), dasatinib, and quercetin (a flavanol found in many plants).

Reducing senescent cell burden can lead to reduced inflammation, decreased macromolecular dysfunction, and enhanced function of stem cells. Adult stem cells also become dysfunctional with age, displaying evidence of senescence.

Senolytics target these senescent cells, preventing them from building up as quickly and slowing down the aging process on a cellular level within the body, thus promoting the proper function of tissues and organs within the body.

In a mouse model, the removal of senescent cells by senolytics in one study resulted in an 36 percent increase in life span, and studies are currently ongoing to test the effects of senolytics on humans. It is likely that by removing the inflammatory impact of senescent cells around the body, we can significantly reduce the aches and pains of old age. It's not a huge leap to predict that removal of these cells will support a longer human lifespan.

Fisetin

One of the most potent senolytics, is the flavonoid fisetin, a natural compound found in many fruits and vegetables including apples, persimmon, grapes, onions, cucumbers and especially strawberries (and who doesn't want to eat more of those?)[6]

Senescent cells are resistant to apoptosis (planned cell death), but in studies fisetin reduced markers of senescence and senescence-associated secretory phenotype (SASPs) in many types of tissues.

The Mayo clinic is currently undertaking clinical trials using fisetin in older adults to evaluate its effect. Interestingly they are also studying fisetin for its effect against COVID. It is suggested that fisetin's senolytic function clears out senescent immune cells, which accumulate with as we age and may be a reason why our older population react so poorly to viruses compared with the younger population.

Fisetin may help prevent COVID-19 from binding to our cells. If this is the case, then it could be a key molecule in the fight against the virus and an indication that clearing senescent cells from the body is an intelligent strategy for improving our overall health and health span. I await the results of this research within interest.

In Summary

In our fifties:

- Exercise!!
- Stimulate autophagy through supplementation including compounds like Withaferin A and Berberine.
- Consider intermittent fasting on a weekly basis.
- Consider taking a natural senolytic, especially fisetin

Chapter 27

The Anti-Aging Power of Exercise

The simplest way to improve our health span is exercise. More than any other intervention, regular physical activity is one of the most effective ways to reduce your risk factors for chronic diseases of aging and improve your health and life span. Earlier we mentioned that our genes have barely changed from our hunter-gatherer forebears. Hunter-gatherers expended a huge amount of energy in daily life simply to survive—finding food and water, seeking shelter, socializing, fleeing sabre-tooth tigers, and so forth.[1]

Demanding days, alternated with rest days and their pattern of physical activity combined aerobic endurance, with flexibility and strength. These are the patterns that remain in our genes and are the ones that our bodies positively respond to - moderate and varied exercise with sufficient time for rest and recuperation.

Regrettably, due to the incredible speed of technological progress over the last two centuries, our core biology remains identical to our Stone-Age ancestors, yet we are living in a vastly different world where we are over-fed, sedentary and chronically stressed. This misalignment from our inborn activity needs is a major cause of the chronic diseases that so many of us suffer, especially as we age.

It makes sense if you consider our brains are wired for energy conservation. We preserve our energy and strength for necessary tasks down to the cellular level. However, our metabolism's wiring to take the path of least resistance plays a major role in the health woes of modern humans because our brain is operating in survival mode in a world of abundance.

Furthermore, a large body of scientific evidence confirms that physical inactivity is a major risk in the development of many chronic diseases, including obesity, insulin resistance, type 2 diabetes, heart disease, and high blood pressure.[2]

If there is one thing you must do to age well, it is regular exercise. It benefits us in so many ways-such as reducing the risk of chronic disease, improving the strength of our muscles and bones, and bolstering our mental health.

But there is good news and a solution. Regular exercise that incorporates our hunter-gatherer patterns reduces the risk of non-communicable disease and is easily achieved through leisure activities and sports.

Humans were built to move and the impact of a lack of exercise on our bodies is extraordinary. If we don't move or exercise, within two days our muscles have already begun to atrophy. A few days of a sedentary lifestyle are sufficient to cause muscle loss, damage to the connection between our muscles and brain, and loss of nerve supply. It can also increase insulin resistance, decreased aerobic capacity, add to fat deposition and aggravate low-grade systemic inflammation.[3]

Physical activity helps prevent excess body fat and results in lower rates of obesity. One of the major contributing factors to the loss of strength and power as we age is a loss of muscle mass. It is an important indicator of how well we are aging, with those with a high muscle mass generally living longer. Furthermore, people who train throughout their life have greater muscle strength compared to sedentary people. As well as muscle mass, they also seemed to be protected against the progressive muscle denervation that is part of the aging process and worsened by inactivity.[4]

Our bones and muscles need the constant stimulation of movement and weight-bearing to build our muscles, and if it stops, then our muscles begin to weaken. In other words, when it comes to muscle mass, use it, or lose it.

The Negative Effects of Sitting

Where this has become dire is in our modern life, where we wake up, roll out of bed, get in our cars, spending a day sitting behind a desk, then come home to sit in front of the tv or computer screen before getting back in bed. This has become even worse with so many people home-bound during the COVID-19 pandemic.

Sitting all day is one of the worst activities for our health, but also one that many people find difficult to avoid. Sedentary activities such as desk work, TV viewing and sitting have an enormous impact on our health and put us at a high risk of disease and even death.

The impact of sitting, however, can be mitigated by taking two-minute walking breaks every 20 or 30 minutes. In fact, a growing body of data shows that the benefits of moderate exercise, with walking several miles a week as good for us as jogging.[5]

Our bodies are genetically adapted to respond well to a diverse range of activities, performed intermittently, at moderate intensities and moderate durations. Even in highly trained individuals, high-intensity, long endurance exercise effort can damage our heart and connective tissue.

Perhaps the biggest advantage of exercise is that it boosts other health interventions that help us age better and buffer our bodies from the effects of eating too much food, well as many other benefits:

- It causes positive epigenetic changes to our DNA and helps restore positive epigenetic patterns
- It reduces chronic inflammation and accumulation of senescent cells
- It improves our cardiovascular health
- Regular exercise is associated with a lower risk of cancer and it encourages mitochondrial biogenesis
- It rejuvenates skeletal muscle stem cells
- It helps maintain telomere length and boosts SIRTUIN activity.
- It boosts production of Brain Derived Neurotropic Factor (BDNF), which promotes mental health and resistance to neurological disorders.

The scientific evidence is overwhelming that our lifestyle choices have a powerful influence on our lifespan, and that regular exercise and physical activity has positive effects on our health. There is boundless fitness and health advice available to us, but the foremost thing we need to do is commit to moving every day. Even a 30 minute walk every day makes an immense difference. It's use it or lose it, so start moving!

Chapter 28
Your Life-Long Longevity Protocol

In your 20s

Exercise, eat a moderate diet, learn how to manage stress.

In your 30s

Exercise, eat a moderate diet, moderate your stress.

Start to be mindful about your future health and focus on the first three primary Hallmarks of Aging and supplement with products that maintain your DNA, including telomere support and methyl donor support.

In your 40s

Continue to exercise, consider incorporating fasting into your lifestyle along with a moderate diet and maintain stress management strategies.

Continue to supplement to protect DNA and healthy gene function. Add to your supplement stack NAD boosters, SIRTUIN activators and other supplements like astaxanthin to boost mitochondrial function and give your cells more energy for repair and maintenance, support your stem cell populations and support healthy levels of intercellular communication.

In your 50s and Beyond

Continue to exercise, in addition to supplements to support your DNA and mitochondria, incorporate strategies such as fasting and certain supplements to stimulate autophagy to clear out senescent cells, repair faulty proteins and cell components and stimulate stem cell renewal.

A summary of actions, interventions and supplements to help support and slow the 9 Hallmarks of Aging.

Hallmark	Priority	Age 20	30-39	40-49	50+
Genomic instability		x	x	x	x
Telomere attrition		x	x	x	x
Epigenetic alterations		x	x	x	x
Mitochondrial dysfunction				x	x
Stem cell fatigue				x	x
Intercellular communication				x	x
Cellular senescence					x
Loss of proteostasis					x
Deregulated nutrient sensing					x

Hallmark	Intervention
Genomic instability	Exercise, non-smoking, moderate diet, moderate to no alcohol consumption
Telomere attrition	Reduce stress (mindfulness and mediation can slow telomere shortening)
Epigenetic alterations	Include foods rich in folate (leafy greens) in your diet
Mitochondrial dysfunction	Reduce avoid certain medicines that affect mitochondrial function, exercise regularly
Stem cell fatigue	Eat a wide range of foods that contain different flavonoids (eat the rainbow of organic fruit and vegetables)
Intercellular communication	Exercise, non-smoking, moderate diet, moderate alcohol consumption
Cellular senescence	Exercise and the range of different fasting methods that support the removal of senescent cells from the body
Loss of proteostasis	Exercise and the range of different fasting methods that support the removal of senescent cells from the body
Deregulated nutrient sensing	Exercise and the range of different fasting methods that support the removal of senescent cells from the body

Supplements	
Supplements that support DNA repair mechanisms	NR, NMN, 2-Hoba, Resveratrol, Pterostilbene, rutin + Vitamin C, Vitamin D, selenium and zinc
Supplements that support telomere length and reduced oxidative stress in the cells	Astragaloside A, astaxanthin, resveratrol, pterostilbene
Supplements that deliver methyl groups to your cells or support key enzymes involved in methylation	5methytetrahydrofolate, SAMe, Curcumin + Vit C
Supplement with NAD boosting compounds and those that support optimal mitochondrial function	NR, NMN, apigenin, rutin, quercetin, astaxanthin, B Vitamins, Carnosine, Alpha Lipoic Acid
Supplement with concentrated flavanoid compounds and supplements that support mitochondrial function	NR, NMN, apigenin, rutin, quercetin, astaxanthin, B Vitamins, carnosine, Alpha Lipoic Acid
Supplement with NAD boosting compounds	Olueropein, astragaloside A, withaferin A, NMN, apigenin
Supplement with compounds known to moderately inhibit mTor and activate AMPK to mimic calorie restriction and trigger autophagy	Berberine, withaferin A, ECGC, fisetin
Supplement with compounds known to moderately inhibit mTor and activate AMPK to mimic calorie restriction and trigger autophagy	Oleuropein, berberine, withaferin A, fisetin, ECGC
Supplement with compounds known to moderately inhibit mTor and activate AMPK to mimic calorie restriction and trigger autophagy	Berberine, withaferin A, ECGC, fisetin

Final Comment

Thanks for making it this far. It's an exciting time in health to capitalize on the massive amount of knowledge being captured by researchers as we start to fully understand the mechanisms in our cells that are involved in aging.

The future of aging will be redefined over the next few decades, and what was an impossible dream only 10 years ago is now starting to become possible. Scientist such as like Valter Longo, David Sinclair and a host of other thought leaders are now guiding us towards a future where we age with ease and grace, capturing the wisdom and mastery of aging without the side effects of disease. At some time in our near future, we will reach escape velocity and transition to homo *sapien longavidas*–long living humans, at which point society will change for ever. How we, as a species, will act when we have full control over our own biology will dictate what that new world will look like and is something for the philosophers to give some serious consideration.

Until then, now is the time for you to start so that you keep your body and your cells in the best condition possible. The single best thing you can do today is to start moving and keep moving. Put aside 30 minutes to walk, even if it is only few times per week, but ultimately work towards a daily habit. Add in listening to a podcast or an audiobook on a subject that interests you while you walk, and you will get double the benefit as you exercise your brain. Or go with a friend so that you benefit from the social connections that we know add years to our lives.

Consider reducing the level of meat in your diet–even one meal a week is going to benefit you and the environment. Imagine if everyone shifted to 3-4 meat free meals a week. The impact on your health and the planet would be considerable.

Also consider adding fasting to your weekly regimen. Not only will you trigger health benefits, but you will reduce your weekly food spend. Missing the breakfast and/or lunch a few times a week looks great on your waistline and is good for your savings account. Or put the money saved towards consuming more organic foods that are much richer in health giving flavonoids and polyphenols than non-organic forms.

And consider adding supplements that naturally boost the levels and activities of key repair and maintenance pathways that we all have running at full capacity when we are young but decline with age. Boosting these pathways creates a virtuous cycle of health for your cells and has a compounding effect on all the other healthy activities you are doing. By doing so, you will boost your chances of arriving at old age with health, vitality and all going well, at a time when medical advances will allow you to further slow and even reverse the aging process.

In our near future, the axioms that "youth is wasted on the young" and that "if I knew now what I did when I was younger" will no longer stand. You will be young, and you will have the benefit of the wisdom and mastery that age brings. This new world will transform society and create a world that will benefit from our collective wisdom and take us towards an exciting but very different future.

Lastly, join me at theninehallmarksofaging.com. New information is coming to light almost daily regarding the aging process and what we can do to slow the process down. It's my mission to curate and share with you what I learn so that I can help as many people on this planet as possible lead a life well lived.

A Global Health Project

Are you interested in advancing human health?

As I worked on this book it became abundantly clear that although our knowledge around our biology, our aging and the impact of health interventions like diet and exercise, supplements and lifestyle is advancing at pace there is still a significant lack of knowledge about what is actually working in terms of combinations of activities and health interventions. And what works for me might not work as well for you.

We know the basics like diet and exercise are beneficial, but what if we add in some mindfulness, supplements or some medicines and then mix it up with different ages, genders or co-existing disease?

Some of the supplements that you are taking alongside all your other activities could be slowing your aging or not helping at all. Would it be useful to you to know that what you are spending your hard-earned money on is working or not?

Perhaps you have a condition like multiple sclerosis and are trying certain interventions to help limit its progress. There will be many people getting it right and possibly many more spending money and committing to activities that are simply not helping.

The Global Health Project is an open-source project that is designed to solve the problem of understanding what is working and what is not across the range of human ages, cultures, races and disease types. By working together and sharing the health data captured by your phone, your fitness trackers and other electronic health devices we can, through the use of artificial intelligence and machine learning, start to identify the interventions that are working the best for people like you and people like me and give us insight that can feed into a wider understanding of what works.

Pop on over to **theninehallmarksofaging.com** to learn more and get involved. It's a collective project and what we learn will be owned by the people involved, so it's a chance to contribute and ultimately benefit as new knowledge is uncovered.

To support this initiative, I will be donating the proceeds from this book to the project.

Lastly, I wish you all the best on your journey to a longer health span. We all have different journeys–some harder than others–but regardless of where you sit and what hands you are dealt with respect to your health, we can always take small steps to improve our health and have more time on this planet to share with our loved ones.

Wishing you a long and healthy life.

Greg Macpherson.

REFERENCES

CHAPTER 1–*How Long Can We Live?*

1 US Center For Disease Control: https://www.cdc.gov/nchs/data-visualization/life-expectancy/

2 https://www.scientificamerican.com/article/theres-no-limit-to-longevity-says-study-reviving-human-life-span-debate/

3 http://supercentenarian-research-foundation.org/TableE.aspx

4 Vijg J, Le Bourg E. Aging and the Inevitable Limit to Human Life Span. Gerontology

5 Sinclair, D. A., & LaPlante, M. D. (2019). Lifespan: Why We Age–and Why We Don't Have To. Atria Books.

6 Riley, J. C. (2005). Estimates of regional and global life expectancy, 1800–2001. Population and development review, 31(3), 537-543.

7 https://ourworldindata.org/child-mortality-global-overview

8 https://ourworldindata.org/child-mortality

9 Andrasfay T, Goldman N. Reductions in 2020 US life expectancy due to COVID-19 and the disproportionate impact on the Black and Latino populations. medRxiv [Preprint]. 2020 Sep 15:2020.07.12.20148387. doi: 10.1101/2020.07.12.20148387. Update in: Proc Natl Acad Sci U S A. 2021 Feb 2;118(5): PMID: 32995806; PMCID: PMC7523145.

10 Fontana L. Modulating human aging and age-associated diseases. Biochim Biophys Acta. 2009 Oct;1790(10):1133-8. doi: 10.1016/j.bbagen.2009.02.002. Epub 2009 Feb 10. PMID: 19364477; PMCID: PMC2829866.

11 Sebastiani, P., & Perls, T. T. (2012). The genetics of extreme longevity: lessons from the new England centenarian study. *Frontiers in genetics*, 3, 277. https://doi.org/10.3389/fgene.2012.00277

12 Vaupel, J. W., & Jeune, B. (1995). The emergence and proliferation of centenarians. *In Exceptional longevity: From prehistory to the present* (pp. 109-116). Odense University Press.

13 Sebastiani, P., & Perls, T. T. (2012). The genetics of extreme longevity: lessons from the new England centenarian study. *Frontiers in genetics*, 3, 277. https://doi.org/10.3389/fgene.2012.00277

14 Nations, U. (2017). World population prospects: the 2017 revision, key findings and advance tables. Department of Economics and Social Affairs PD, editor. New York: United Nations

15 United Nations, Department of Economic and Social Affairs, Population Division (2019). World Population Prospects 2019, Online Edition. Rev. 1.

CHAPTER 2–*Closing the Gap*

1 Eileen M. Crimmins, Lifespan and Healthspan: Past, Present, and Promise, The Gerontologist, Volume 55, Issue 6, December 2015, Pages 901–911, https://doi.org/10.1093/geront/gnv130

2 https://www.who.int/gho/mortality_burden_disease/ life_tables/hale_text/en/

3 https://www.who.int/gho/mortality_burden_disease/ life_tables/hale_text/en/

4 Brown G. C. (2015). Living too long: the current focus of medical research on increasing the quantity, rather than the quality, of life is damaging our health and harming the economy. EMBO reports, 16(2), 137–141. 8

5 GBD 2017 Disease and Injury Incidence and Prevalence Collaborators (2018). Global, regional, and national incidence, prevalence, and years lived with disability for 354 diseases and injuries for 195 countries and territories, 1990-2017: a systematic analysis for the Global Burden of Disease Study 2017. Lancet (London, England), 392(10159), 1789–1858.

6 https://www.healthsystemtracker.org/chart-collection/health-expenditures-vary-across-population

CHAPTER 3–*How We Die Now*

1 https://ourworldindata.org/burden-of-disease

2 Centers for Disease Control and Prevention (CDC). Control of infectious diseases. MMWR Morb Mortal Wkly Rep. 1999 Jul 30;48(29):621-9. PMID: 10458535.

3 Mitchell SW. *Wear and Tear, or Hints for the Overworked.* 5th ed. Philadelphia, Pa: JB Lippincott; 1887.

4 Jones, David S., Scott H. Podolsky, and Jeremy A. Greene. 2012. "The Burden of Disease and the Changing Task of Medicine." New England Journal of Medicine 366 (25) (June 21): 2333–2338.

5 https://www.cdc.gov/smallpox/history/history.html

6 Noakes, T. D., Borresen, J., Hew-Butler, T., Lambert, M. I., & Jordaan, E. (2008). Semmelweis and the aetiology of puerperal sepsis 160 years on: an historical review. *Epidemiology and infection*, 136(1), 1–9. https://doi.org/10.1017/S0950268807008746

CHAPTER 4–*Agism and the Cult of Youth*

1 Cohen, P. (2012). *In our prime: The invention of middle age.* Simon and Schuster.

2 Chang ES, Kannoth S, Levy S, Wang SY, Lee JE, Levy BR. Global reach of agism on older persons' health: A systematic review. PLoS One. 2020 Jan 15;15(1):e0220857

3 Butler, R. N. (2009). *The longevity revolution: The benefits and challenges of living a long life.* Hachette UK.

4 Levy, B. R., Slade, M. D., Chang, E. S., Kannoth, S., & Wang, S. Y. (2020). Agism Amplifies Cost and Prevalence of Health Conditions. The Gerontologist, 60(1), 174–181

Chapter 5–What Is Aging?

1 López-Otín C, Blasco MA, Partridge L, Serrano M, Kroemer G. The Hallmarks of Aging. Cell. 2013 Jun 6;153(6):1194- 217

2 Bianconi E, Piovesan A, Facchin F, Beraudi A, Casadei R, Frabetti F, Vitale L, Pelleri MC, Tassani S, Piva F, Perez-Amodio S, Strippoli P, Canaider S. An estimation of the number of cells in the human body. Ann Hum Biol. 2013 Nov-Dec;40(6):463-71.

Chapter 6 – Hallmark One–Genomic Instability

1 Noda A, Mishima S, Hirai Y, Hamasaki K, Landes RD, Mitani H, Haga K, Kiyono T, Nakamura N, Kodama Y (2015). "Progerin, the protein responsible for the Hutchinson-Gilford progeria syndrome, increases the unrepaired DNA damages following exposure to ionizing radiation" Genes Environ. 37: 13.

2 Sinclair, D. A., & LaPlante, M. D. (2019). Lifespan: Why We Age–and Why We Don't Have To. Atria Books

3 Sinclair, D. A., & LaPlante, M. D. (2019). Lifespan: Why We Age–and Why We Don't Have To. Atria Books.

4 D. L., & Bohr, V. A. (2015). DNA Damage, DNA Repair, Aging, and Neurodegeneration. Cold Spring Harbor perspectives in medicine, 5(10), a025130.

5 O'Donovan PJ, Livingston DM. BRCA1 and BRCA2: breast/ovarian cancer susceptibility gene products and participants in DNA double-strand break repair. Carcinogenesis. 2010 Jun;31(6):961-7.

6 F. L. (2018). Carcinogens and DNA damage. Biochemical Society transactions, 46(5), 1213–1224.

Chapter 7–Hallmark Two-Telomere Attrition

1 Hayflick L, Moorhead PS (1961). "The serial cultivation of human diploid cell strains". Exp Cell Res. 25 (3): 585–621.

2 Gilchrest BA, Eller MS, Yaar M. Telomere-mediated effects on melanogenesis and skin aging. J Investig Dermatol Symp Proc. 2009 Aug;14(1):25-31.

3 Lapham, K., Kvale, M. N., Lin, J., Connell, S., Croen, L. A., Dispensa, B. P., ... & Jorgenson, E. (2015). Automated assay of telomere length measurement and informatics for 100,000 subjects in the genetic epidemiology research on adult health and aging (GERA) cohort. Genetics, 200(4), 1061-1072.

4 Blackburn, E., & Epel, E. (2017). The telomere effect: a revolutionary approach to living younger, healthier, longer. Hachette UK.

5 Blackburn EH, Greider CW, Szostak JW. Telomeres and telomerase: the path from maize, Tetrahymena and yeast to human cancer and aging. Nat Med. 2006 Oct;12(10):1133-8.

6 Jaskelioff, M., Muller, F., Paik, J. et al. Telomerase reactivation reverses tissue degeneration in aged telomerase-deficient mice. Nature 469, 102–106 (2011). https://doi.org/10.1038/nature09603

CHAPTER 8–HALLMARK THREE–EPIGENETIC ALTERATIONS

1 Barnett, J. H., & Smoller, J. W. (2009). The genetics of bipolar disorder. Neuroscience, 164(1), 331–343.

2 Sachdev PS, Lee T, Wen W, Ames D, Batouli AH, Bowden J, Brodaty H, Chong E, Crawford J, Kang K, Mather K, Lammel A, Slavin MJ, Thalamuthu A, Trollor J, Wright MJ; OATS Research Team. The contribution of twins to the study of cognitive aging and dementia: the Older Australian Twins Study. Int Rev Psychiatry. 2013 Dec;25(6):738-47.

3 Brouwer RM, Panizzon MS, Glahn DC, Hibar DP, Hua X, Jahanshad N, et al. Genetic influences on individual differences in longitudinal changes in global and subcortical brain volumes Results of the ENIGMA plasticity working group. Human Brain Mapping. 2017. 38(9):4444-4458.

4 Grazioli, E., Dimauro, I., Mercatelli, N. et al. Physical activity in the prevention of human diseases: role of epigenetic modifications. BMC Genomics 18, 802 (2017).

5 Cheung, P., Vallania, F., Warsinske, H. C., Donato, M., Schaffert, S., Chang, S. E., Dvorak, M., Dekker, C. L., Davis, M. M., Utz, P. J., Khatri, P., & Kuo, A. J. (2018). Single-Cell Chromatin Modification Profiling Reveals Increased Epigenetic Variations with Aging. *Cell*, 173(6), 1385–1397.e14. https://doi.org/10.1016/j.cell.2018.03.079

6 Grazioli, E., Dimauro, I., Mercatelli, N. et al. Physical activity in the prevention of human diseases: role of epigenetic modifications. BMC Genomics 18, 802 (2017).

7 Lee, I. M., Shiroma, E. J., Lobelo, F., Puska, P., Blair, S. N., Katzmarzyk, P. T., & Lancet Physical Activity Series Working Group (2012). Effect of physical inactivity on major non-communicable diseases worldwide: an analysis of burden of disease and life expectancy. *Lancet (London, England)*, 380(9838), 219–229. 9

8 Radom-Aizik, S., Zaldivar, F., Haddad, F., & Cooper, D. M. (2013). Impact of brief exercise on peripheral blood NK cell gene and microRNA expression in young adults. Journal of applied physiology (Bethesda, Md. : 1985), 114(5), 628–636.

CHAPTER 9– HALLMARK FOUR–LOSS OF PROTEOSTASIS

1 Ponomarenko, E. A., Poverennaya, E. V., Ilgisonis, E. V., Pyatnitskiy, M. A., Kopylov, A. T., Zgoda, V. G., Lisitsa, A. V., & Archakov, A. I. (2016). The Size of the Human Proteome: The Width and Depth. International journal of analytical chemistry, 2016, 7436849.

2 Santra, M., Dill, K. A., & de Graff, A. (2019). Proteostasis collapse is a driver of cell aging and death. Proceedings of the National Academy of Sciences of the United States of America, 116(44), 22173–22178.

3 Rao, R. V., & Bredesen, D. E. (2004). Misfolded proteins, endoplasmic reticulum stress and neurodegeneration. *Current opinion in cell biology*, 16(6), 653–662.

4 GBD 2016 Dementia Collaborators (2019). Global, regional, and national burden of Alzheimer's disease and other dementias, 1990-2016: a systematic analysis for the Global Burden of Disease Study 2016. The Lancet. Neurology, 18(1), 88–106.

5 Hannah Stocker, Andreas Nabers, Laura Perna, Tobias Möllers, Dan Rujescu, Annette Hartmann, Bernd Holleczek, Ben Schöttker, Klaus Gerwert, Hermann Brenner. Prediction of Alzheimer's disease diagnosis within 14 years through Aβ misfolding in blood plasma compared to APOE4 status, and other risk factors. Alzheimer's & Dementia, 2019.

6 Edkins, A. L., Price, J. T., Pockley, A. G., & Blatch, G. L. (2018). Heat shock proteins as modulators and therapeutic targets of chronic disease: an integrated perspective. *Philosophical transactions of the Royal Society of London. Series B, Biological sciences*, 373(1738), 20160521.

CHAPTER 10– HALLMARK FIVE–DEREGULATED NUTRIENT SENSING

7 Wyttenbach, A., & Arrigo, A. P. (2009). The role of heat shock proteins during neurodegeneration in Alzheimer's, Parkinson's and Huntington's disease. In Heat shock proteins in neural cells (pp. 81-99). Springer, New York, NY.

1 McDonald, R. B., & Ramsey, J. J. (2010). Honoring Clive McCay and 75 years of calorie restriction research. The Journal of nutrition, 140(7), 1205–1210.

2 Bettedi, L., & Foukas, L. C. (2017). Growth factor, energy and nutrient sensing signalling pathways in metabolic aging. Biogerontology, 18(6), 913-929.

3 ATP is discussed in depth further along, but essentially our cells break down glucose through a complex process to ATP, which is the main fuel for our cells.

4 Brand-Miller, J. C., Griffin, H. J., & Colagiuri, S. (2012). The carnivore connection hypothesis: revisited. Journal of obesity, 2012, 258624.

5 Leonard WR, Snodgrass JJ, Robertson ML. Effects of brain evolution on human nutrition and metabolism. Annu Rev Nutr. 2007;27:311–27.

6 Leonard WR, Snodgrass JJ, Robertson ML. Effects of brain evolution on human nutrition and metabolism. Annu Rev Nutr. 2007;27:311–27.

7 O'Keefe JH, Vogel R, Lavie CJ, Cordain L. Achieving hunter- gatherer fitness in the 21(st) century: back to the future. Am J Med. 2010 Dec;123(12):1082-6.

8 Colagiuri S, Brand Miller J. The 'carnivore connection'-- evolutionary aspects of insulin resistance. Eur J Clin Nutr. 2002;56 Suppl 1:S30-S35.

9 Linn, T., Santosa, B., Grönemeyer, D., Aygen, S., Scholz, N., Busch, M., & Bretzel, R. G. (2000). Effect of long-term dietary protein intake on glucose metabolism in humans. Diabetologia, 43(10), 1257-1265.

10 SIGMA Type 2 Diabetes Consortium, Williams, A. L., Jacobs, S. B., Moreno-Macías, H., Huerta-Chagoya, A., Churchhouse, C., Márquez-Luna, C., García-Ortíz, H., Gómez-Vázquez, M. J., Burtt, N. P., Aguilar-Salinas, C. A., González-Villalpando, C., Florez, J. C., Orozco, L., Haiman, C. A., Tusié-Luna, T., & Altshuler, D. (2014).

Sequence variants in SLC16A11 are a common risk factor for type 2 diabetes in Mexico. *Nature*, 506(7486), 97–101. https://doi.org/10.1038/nature12828

11 Hales CN, Barker DJ. The thrifty phenotype hypothesis. Br Med Bull. 2001;60:5-20. doi: 10.1093/bmb/60.1.5. PMID: 11809615.

12 Reaven GM. Hypothesis: muscle insulin resistance is the ("not-so") thrifty genotype. Diabetologia. 1998 Apr;41(4):482-4.

1 van den Heuvel J, English S, Uller T. Disposable Soma Theory and the Evolution of Maternal Effects on Aging. PLoS One. 2016 Jan 11;11(1):e0145544.

2 Bettedi, L., & Foukas, L. C. (2017). Growth factor, energy and nutrient sensing signalling pathways in metabolic aging. Biogerontology, 18(6), 913-929.

3 Junnila, R. K., List, E. O., Berryman, D. E., Murrey, J. W., & Kopchick, J. J. (2013). The GH/IGF-1 axis in aging and longevity. *Nature reviews. Endocrinology*, 9(6), 366–376. https://doi.org/10.1038/nrendo.2013.67

4 Rudman D, Feller AG, Nagraj HS, Gergans GA, Lalitha PY, Goldberg AF, Schlenker RA, Cohn L, Rudman IW, Mattson DE. Effects of human growth hormone in men over 60 years old. N England J Med. 1990 Jul 5;323(1):1-6.

5 Blackman MR, Sorkin JD, Münzer T, Bellantoni MF, Busby-Whitehead J, Stevens TE, Jayme J, O'Connor KG, Christmas C, Tobin JD, Stewart KJ, Cottrell E, St Clair C, Pabst KM, Harman SM. Growth hormone and sex steroid administration in healthy aged women and men: a randomized controlled trial. JAMA. 2002 Nov 13;288(18):2282-92.

6 Suh, Y., Atzmon, G., Cho, M. O., Hwang, D., Liu, B., Leahy, D. J., Barzilai, N., & Cohen, P. (2008). Functionally significant insulin- like growth factor I receptor mutations in centenarians. Proceedings of the National Academy of Sciences of the United States of America, 105(9), 3438–3442.

7 Vitale, G., Brugts, M. P., Ogliari, G., Castaldi, D., Fatti, L. M., Varewijck, A. J., Lamberts, S. W., Monti, D., Bucci, L., Cevenini, E., Cavagnini, F., Franceschi, C., Hofland, L. J., Mari, D., & Janssen, J. (2012). Low circulating IGF-I bioactivity is associated with human longevity: findings in centenarians' offspring. Aging, 4(9), 580–589.

8 NCD Risk Factor Collaboration. (2016). Trends in adult body-mass index in 200 countries from 1975 to 2014: a pooled analysis of 1698 population-based measurement studies with 19· 2 million participants. The Lancet, 387(10026), 1377-1396

9 https://www.who.int/en/news-room/fact-sheets/detail/obesity-and-overweight

10 Censin, J. C., Peters, S., Bovijn, J., Ferreira, T., Pulit, S. L., Mägi, R., Mahajan, A., Holmes, M. V., & Lindgren, C. M. (2019). Causal relationships between obesity and the leading causes of death in women and men. PLoS genetics, 15(10), e1008405.

11 Koenig, R. J., Peterson, C. M., Jones, R. L., Saudek, C., Lehrman, M., & Cerami, A. (1976). Correlation of glucose regulation and hemoglobin AIc in diabetes mellitus. New England Journal of Medicine, 295(8), 417-420.

12 Koenig, R. J., Peterson, C. M., Jones, R. L., Saudek, C., Lehrman, M., & Cerami, A. (1976). Correlation of glucose regulation and hemoglobin AIc in diabetes mellitus. New England Journal of Medicine, 295(8), 417-420.

13 Prasad, C., Davis, K. E., Imrhan, V., Juma, S., & Vijayagopal, P. (2017). Advanced Glycation End Products and Risks for Chronic Diseases: Intervening Through Lifestyle Modification. *American journal of lifestyle medicine*, 13(4), 384–404. https://doi.org/10.1177/1559827617708991

1 Raught, B., Gingras, A. C., & Sonenberg, N. (2001). The target of rapamycin (TOR) proteins. *Proceedings of the National Academy of Sciences of the United States of America*, 98(13), 7037–7044. https://doi.org/10.1073/pnas.121145898

2 Carling D. AMPK signalling in health and disease. Curr Opin Cell Biol. 2017 Apr;45:31-37.

CHAPTER 11– HALLMARK SIX–MITOCHONDRIAL DYSFUNCTION

1 Sanz A, Stefanatos RK. The mitochondrial free radical theory of aging: a critical view. Curr Aging Sci. 2008 Mar;1(1):10- 21.

2 Bjelakovic G, Nikolova D, Gluud LL, Simonetti RG, Gluud C. Antioxidant supplements for prevention of mortality in healthy participants and patients with various diseases. Cochrane Database of Systematic Reviews 2012, Issue 3. Art. No.: CD007176

3 Sena, L. A., & Chandel, N. S. (2012). Physiological roles of mitochondrial reactive oxygen species. Molecular cell, 48(2), 158–167. https://doi.org/10.1016/j.molcel.2012.09.025.

Chapter 12– HALLMARK SEVEN–CELLULAR SENESCENCE

1 Xu M., Pirtskhalava T., Farr J.N., Weigand B.M., Palmer A.K., Weivoda M.M. Senolytics improve physical function and increase lifespan in old age. Nat Med. 2018;24:1246–1256

2 Ohtani N. Deciphering the mechanism for induction of senescence-associated secretory phenotype (SASP) and its role in aging and cancer development. J Biochem. 2019 Jul 12:mvz055

3 Mitteldorf J. What Is Antagonistic Pleiotropy? Biochemistry (Mosc). 2019 Dec;84(12):1458-1468.

4 Ungewitter E, Scrable H. Antagonistic pleiotropy and p53. Mech Aging Dev. 2009 Jan-Feb;130(1-2):10-7. doi: 10.1016/j.mad.2008.06.002. Epub 2008 Jul 1. PMID: 18639575; PMCID: PMC2771578.

CHAPTER 13– HALLMARK EIGHT–STEM CELL EXHAUSTION

1 Sender, R., Fuchs, S., & Milo, R. (2016). Revised Estimates for the Number of Human and Bacteria Cells in the Body. *PLoS biology*, 14(8), e1002533. https://doi.org/10.1371/journal.pbio.1002533

2 Gattazzo, F., Urciuolo, A., & Bonaldo, P. (2014). Extracellular matrix: a dynamic microenvironment for stem cell niche. Biochimica et biophysica acta, 1840(8), 2506–2519.

3 Macaluso F, Myburgh KH. Current evidence that exercise can increase the number of adult stem cells. J Muscle Res Cell Motil. 2012 Aug;33(3-4):187-98. doi: 10.1007/s10974-012-9302-0. Epub 2012 Jun 7. PMID: 22673936.

4 Brandhorst, S., Choi, I. Y., Wei, M., Cheng, C. W., Sedrakyan, S., Navarrete, G., Dubeau, L., Yap, L. P., Park, R., Vinciguerra, M., Di Biase, S., Mirzaei, H., Mirisola, M. G., Childress, P., Ji, L., Groshen, S., Penna, F., Odetti, P., Perin, L., Conti, P. S., ... Longo, V. D. (2015). A Periodic Diet that Mimics Fasting Promotes Multi-System Regeneration, Enhanced Cognitive Performance, and Healthspan. Cell metabolism, 22(1), 86–99.

CHAPTER 14– HALLMARK NINE–ALTERED INTERCELLULAR COMMUNICATION

1 Sender, R., Fuchs, S., & Milo, R. (2016). Revised estimates for the number of human and bacteria cells in the body. PLoS biology, 14(8), e1002533.

2 https://nextstrain.org/flu/seasonal/h3n2/ha/2y?l=clock

3 Smith AG, Sheridan PA, Harp JB, Beck MA. Diet-induced obese mice have increased mortality and altered immune responses when infected with influenza virus. J Nutr. 2007 May;137(5):1236-43.

4 Boutens, L., & Stienstra, R. (2016). Adipose tissue macrophages: going off track during obesity. *Diabetologia*, 59(5), 879–894. https://doi.org/10.1007/s00125-016-3904-9

CHAPTER 15– *It's Never Too Soon or Too Late to Start*

1 Buettner, D., & Skemp, S. (2016). Blue Zones: Lessons From the World's Longest Lived. *American journal of lifestyle medicine*, 10(5), 318–321. https://doi.org/10.1177/1559827616637066

1 AGE LATER. Health Span, Life Span, and the New Science of Longevity. Nir Barzilai, M.D.

2 Tanaka M, Gong J, Zhang J, Yamada Y, Borgeld HJ, Yagi K. Mitochondrial genotype associated with longevity and its inhibitory effect on mutagenesis. Mech Aging Dev. 2000 Jul 31;116(2-3):65- 76.

3 Khan SS, Shah SJ, Klyachko E, Baldridge AS, Eren M, Place AT, Aviv A, Puterman E, Lloyd-Jones DM, Heiman M, Miyata T, Gupta S, Shapiro AD, Vaughan DE. A null mutation in SERPINE1 protects against biological aging in humans. Sci Adv. 2017 Nov 15;3(11):eaao1617.

4 Herskind AM, McGue M, Holm NV, Sørensen TI, Harvald B, Vaupel JW. The heritability of human longevity: a population-based study of 2872 Danish twin pairs born 1870-1900. Hum Genet. 1996 Mar;97(3):319-23.

5 Franco, M., Bilal, U., Orduñez, P., Benet, M., Morejón, A., Caballero, B., Kennelly, J.F. & Cooper, R.S. (2013) Population-wide weight loss and regain in relation to diabetes burden and cardiovascular mortality in Cuba 1980-2010: repeated cross sectional surveys and ecological comparison of secular trends. BMJ.

6 Martin CK, Bhapkar M, Pittas AG, Pieper CF, Das SK, Williamson DA, Scott T, Redman LM, Stein R, Gilhooly CH, Stewart T, Robinson L, Roberts SB; Comprehensive Assessment of Long- term Effects of Reducing Intake of Energy (CALERIE) Phase 2 Study Group. Effect of Calorie Restriction on Mood, Quality of Life, Sleep, and Sexual Function in Healthy Nonobese Adults: The CALERIE 2 Randomized Clinical Trial. JAMA Intern Med. 2016 Jun 1;176(6):743-52.

7 Dorling JL, Das SK, Racette SB, Apolzan JW, Zhang D, Pieper CF, Martin CK; CALERIE Study Group. Changes in body weight, adherence, and appetite during 2 years of calorie restriction: the CALERIE 2 randomized clinical trial. Eur J Clin Nutr. 2020 Aug;74(8):1210-1220. doi: 10.1038/s41430-020-0593-8. Epub 2020 Mar 6. PMID: 32144378; PMCID: PMC7415503.

8 Kalm, L. M., & Semba, R. D. (2005). They starved so that others be better fed: remembering Ancel Keys and the Minnesota experiment. *The Journal of nutrition*, 135(6), 1347-1352.

Chapter 16– A Whole Life Approach

1 Heijmans BT, Tobi EW, Stein AD, Putter H, Blauw GJ, Susser ES, Slagboom PE, Lumey LH. Persistent epigenetic differences associated with prenatal exposure to famine in humans. Proc Natl Acad Sci U S A. 2008 Nov 4;105(44):17046-9. doi: 10.1073/pnas.0806560105. Epub 2008 Oct 27. PMID: 18955703; PMCID: PMC2579375.

2 See Chapter 16 Boost DNA Repair Systems

CHAPTER 18– *Build Your Healthy Aging Life Plan*

1 Hogan, K. A., Chini, C., & Chini, E. N. (2019). The Multi-faceted Ecto-enzyme CD38: Roles in Immunomodulation, Cancer, Aging, and Metabolic Diseases. Frontiers in immunology, 10, 1187.

2 Williams RJ, Spencer JP, Rice-Evans C. Flavonoids: antioxidants or signalling molecules? Free Radic Biol Med. 2004;36(7):838-849.

3 Escande, C., Nin, V., Price, N. L., Capellini, V., Gomes, A. P., Barbosa, M. T., O'Neil, L., White, T. A., Sinclair, D. A., & Chini, E. N. (2013). Flavonoid apigenin is an inhibitor of the NAD+ ase CD38: implications for cellular NAD+ metabolism, protein acetylation, and treatment of metabolic syndrome. *Diabetes*, 62(4), 1084–1093. https://doi.org/10.2337/db12-1139

CHAPTER 19–*Maintain Telomere Length*

1 Blackburn, E., & Epel, E. (2017). *The telomere effect: a revolutionary approach to living younger, healthier, longer*. Hachette UK.

2 Tsoukalas, D., Fragkiadaki, P., Docea, A. O., Alegakis, A. K., Sarandi, E., Thanasoula, M., Spandidos, D. A., Tsatsakis, A., Razgonova, M. P., & Calina, D. (2019). Discovery of potent telomerase activators: Unfolding new therapeutic and anti-aging perspectives. Molecular medicine reports, 20(4), 3701–3708.

CHAPTER 20– *Epigenetic Alterations and Protein Repair*

1 Brandhorst, S., Choi, I. Y., Wei, M., Cheng, C. W., Sedrakyan, S., Navarrete, G., Dubeau, L., Yap, L. P., Park, R., Vinciguerra, M., Di Biase, S., Mirzaei, H., Mirisola, M. G., Childress, P., Ji, L., Groshen, S., Penna, F., Odetti, P., Perin, L., Conti, P. S., ... Longo, V. D. (2015). A Periodic Diet that Mimics Fasting Promotes Multi-System Regeneration, Enhanced Cognitive Performance, and Healthspan. Cell metabolism, 22(1), 86–99

1 Eliopoulos, A. G., Havaki, S., & Gorgoulis, V. G. (2016). DNA Damage Response and Autophagy: A Meaningful Partnership. Frontiers in genetics, 7, 204.

CHAPTER 21– *Calorie Restriction and Longevity*

2 Picca, A., Pesce, V., & Lezza, A. (2017). Does eating less make you live longer and better? An update on calorie restriction. Clinical interventions in aging, 12, 1887–1902.

3 Solon-Biet SM, McMahon AC, Ballard JW, Ruohonen K, Wu LE, Cogger VC, Warren A, Huang X, Pichaud N, Melvin RG, Gokarn R, Khalil M, Turner N, Cooney GJ, Sinclair DA, Raubenheimer D, Le Couteur DG, Simpson SJ. The ratio of macronutrients, not caloric intake, dictates cardiometabolic health, aging, and longevity in ad libitum-fed mice. Cell Metab. 2014 Mar 4;19(3):418-30.

4 Aliper A, Jellen L, Cortese F, Artemov A, Karpinsky-Semper D, Moskalev A, Swick AG, Zhavoronkov A. Towards natural mimetics of metformin and rapamycin. Aging (Albany NY). 2017 Nov 15;9(11):2245-2268.

CHAPTER 23– *Replenishing Stem Cells*

CHAPTER 24– *Reducing Cellular Senescence and Inflammation*

5 Ellison-Hughes G. M. (2020). First evidence that senolytics are effective at decreasing senescent cells in humans. EBioMedicine, 56, 102473.

6 Yousefzadeh, M. J., Zhu, Y., McGowan, S. J., Angelini, L., Fuhrmann-Stroissnigg, H., Xu, M., Ling, Y. Y., Melos, K. I., Pirtskhalava, T., Inman, C. L., McGuckian, C., Wade, E. A., Kato, J. I., Grassi, D., Wentworth, M., Burd, C. E., Arriaga, E. A., Ladiges, W. L., Tchkonia, T., Kirkland, J. L., … Niedernhofer, L. J. (2018). Fisetin is a senotherapeutic that extends health and lifespan. EBioMedicine, 36, 18–28.

CHAPTER 25– *The Anti-Aging Power of Exercise*

1 O'Keefe, J. H., Vogel, R., Lavie, C. J., & Cordain, L. (2010). Achieving hunter-gatherer fitness in the 21st century: back to the future. *The American journal of medicine*, 123(12), 1082-1086.

2 Atherton, P. J., Greenhaff, P. L., Phillips, S. M., Bodine, S. C., Adams, C. M., & Lang, C. H. (2016). Control of skeletal muscle atrophy in response to disuse: clinical/preclinical contentions and fallacies of evidence. American journal of physiology. Endocrinology and metabolism, 311(3), E594–E604.

3 Narici M, De Vito G, Franchi M, Paoli A, Moro T, Marcolin G, Grassi B, Baldassarre G, Zuccarelli L, Biolo G, di Girolamo FG, Fiotti N, Dela F, Greenhaff P, Maganaris C. Impact of sedentarism due to the COVID-19 home confinement on neuromuscular, cardiovascular and metabolic health: Physiological and pathophysiological implications and recommendations for physical and nutritional countermeasures. Eur J Sport Sci. 2020 May 12:1-22.

4 Harridge SD, Lazarus NR. Physical Activity, Aging, and Physiological Function. Physiology (Bethesda). 2017 Mar;32(2):152-161. doi: 10.1152/physiol.00029.2016. PMID: 28228482.

5 Bouchard C, Blair SN, Katzmarzyk PT. Less Sitting, More Physical Activity, or Higher Fitness? Mayo Clin Proc. 2015 Nov;90(11):1533-40.

Made in United States
Orlando, FL
06 September 2022

22064365R00135